Issues and Beliefs in the
CATHOLIC FAITH

MIKE KEENE

Hodder & Stoughton

A MEMBER OF THE HODDER HEADLINE GROUP

ACKNOWLEDGEMENTS

The publishers would like to thank the following for permission to reproduce copyright material in this volume:

Cassell-Geoffrey Chapman (UK) for extracts from the *New Catechism of the Catholic Church*, 1994.

The publishers would also like to thank the following individuals, institutions and companies for permission to reproduce copyright illustrations in this book:

Alex Keene for supplying all the photographs used, with exception to the following: page 35: reproduced with kind permission from CAFOD; page 41: Bettmann/CORBIS; page 43: Hulton Getty; page 55: Christa Stadtler/Photofusion, David King Collection; page 65: Time Page/CORBIS; page 67: Imperial War Museum; page 91: Richard Cummins/CORBIS; page 99 (bottom right): Ute Klaphake/Photofusion, David King Collection; page 119: Jennie Woodcock; Reflections Photolibrary/CORBIS.

NOTE: Throughout the book the abbreviations BCE (Before Common Era) and CE (Common Era) are used. They have the same meaning as the more familiar BC and AD. The *Catechism of the Catholic Church* is referred to as CCC; numbers in brackets are paragraph references.

The Biblical text used is the New International Version, Hodder & Stoughton (1973).

Orders: please contact Bookpoint Ltd, 78 Milton Park, Abingdon, Oxon OX14 4TD. Telephone: (44) 01235 827720, Fax: (44) 01235 400454. Lines are open from 9.00 – 6.00, Monday to Saturday, with a 24 hour message answering service. Email address: orders@bookpoint.co.uk

British Library Cataloguing in Publication Data
A catalogue record for this title is available from The British Library

ISBN 0 340 774789

First published 2000
Impression number   10   9   8   7   6   5   4   3   2   1
Year   2005   2004   2003   2002   2001   2000

Cover photo: Images copyright © 1999 PhotoDisc.
Typeset by Wearset, Boldon, Tyne and Wear
Printed in Italy for Hodder & Stoughton Educational, a division of Hodder Headline Plc, 338 Euston Road, London NW1 3BH by Printer Trento

CONTENTS

1 CHRISTIAN VALUES

1.1 WHAT ARE CHRISTIAN VALUES?

KEY QUESTION

What are the basic cardinal and theological virtues?

Extract 1

Love is patient, love is kind. It does not envy, it does not boast, it is not proud. It is not rude, it is not self-seeking, it is not easily angered, it keeps no record of wrongs. Love does not delight in evil but rejoices in the truth. It always protects, always trusts, always hopes, always preserves. Love never fails . . . And now these three remain: faith, hope and love. But the greatest of these is love.

1 Corinthians 13:4–8;13

Extract 2

Love is itself the fulfilment of all our works. There is the goal; that is why we run: we run toward it, and once we reach it, in it we shall find rest.

St Augustine

There is a close link in the Christian faith between belief and action. The most important beliefs that a Christian holds are focused on Jesus Christ, Lord and Saviour. Christianity, however, is much more than a set of beliefs – it is a way of life. Alone of all creatures, human beings have been given an eternal soul and this is where the intellect and will are located.

- Our intellect gives us the capacity to recognise, and understand, God's command to do good and avoid evil.
- Our free will enables us to respond to the promptings of our conscience and to God's law of love. It is only in loving truth and goodness that human beings are able to find true happiness.

Both our intellect and our will need to be educated to seek the good. The Catholic Church and the Scriptures are two of the most important educators. The Scriptures, in particular, provide clear guidance as to where the good and true happiness are to be found, notably in:

- the Ten Commandments (see 1.2 and 1.3)
- the Beatitudes (see 1.4 and 1.5)
- the Sermon on the Mount (see 1.6 and 1.7).

The cardinal virtues

A 'virtue' is a habit which turns our ideals and beliefs into everyday actions. It is a firm intention to live a good life. Human virtues govern our actions and help us to control our passions and feelings. The four 'cardinal' (basic) virtues listed below are the source of all the good habits by which we live. Between them they guide our intellects and wills. They enable us to live lives that are pleasing to God.

1 Prudence   This is the wisdom that we need to see the proper course of action to take – and the strength to take it.

2 Justice   Through this virtue God, and human beings, receive what rightfully belongs to them.

3 Fortitude   This is the courage and strength to do what is right – especially when temptations and fears have to be overcome first.

4 Temperance   This moderates and controls our passions so that we are able to live a Christ-like life.

The theological virtues

These three virtues are mentioned by Paul (see Extract 1) as being those that link us with God himself. They are the foundation of every Christian moral life.

1 Faith   This brings us to believe in the God who is truth and is made known to us through the Church and the Scriptures. Faith then develops our relationship with the God of truth. The true Christian is one who believes the truth and translates it into action in everyday life.

2 Hope   Hope encourages us to trust in God's promise of salvation by keeping us from despair and enabling us to believe that we will reach heaven. The Beatitudes provide the foundation for this hope.

3 Charity   Charity (love) is the basis of the Christian life. Love is a gift from God and actively shows itself towards God and our neighbours. Love unites us to the three members of the Trinity:
- God, who is the source of all love
- Jesus, who showed us God's love in all that he did
- the Holy Spirit, who gives us the strength to love.

Jesus left his disciples with one command: 'Love one another as I have loved you' (John 15:12). This law is God's basic requirement. By loving we show that we are children of God.

WORK TO DO

1 a) What is a virtue?
   b) What are the four cardinal virtues?
   c) Why do you think that the cardinal virtues are very important for every Catholic?

2 a) What are the theological virtues?
   b) How would you explain the importance of the theological virtues to someone who wanted to be a follower of Jesus?

Extract 3

It is not easy for man, wounded by sin, to maintain moral balance. Christ's gift of salvation offers us the grace necessary to persevere in the pursuit of the virtues. Everyone should always ask for this grace of light and strength, frequent the sacraments, co-operate with the Holy Spirit, and follow his calls to love what is good and shun evil.

CCC (1811)

DISCUSSION POINT

How would you recognise a life lived by the virtues of faith, hope and charity?

KEY WORDS

Beatitudes
Disciples
Paul
Sermon on the Mount
Ten Commandments
Trinity

Why is education in the Catholic faith important for all Roman Catholics?

1.2 THE TEN COMMANDMENTS (1)

KEY QUESTION

What do the first three commandments say and what is their relevance to the Christian today?

CONSULT

Exodus 20:1–11

Extract 1

Jesus replied: 'Love the Lord your God with all your heart and with all your soul and with all your mind. This is the first and greatest commandment. And the second is like it: love your neighbour as yourself. All the Law and the Prophets hang on these two commandments.'

Matthew 22:37–40

Extract 2

Lifting up the mind towards God is an expression of our adoration of God: prayer of praise and thanksgiving, intercession and petition. Prayer is an indispensable condition for being able to obey God's commandments.

CCC (2098)

The CCC devotes a lengthy chapter to the Ten Commandments, showing that these ancient laws, given by God to Moses on Mount Sinai, have always played an important part in the teaching of the Catholic Church. They express 'grave obligations' which show people's responsibility towards God (Commandments 1–3) and their neighbours (Commandments 4–10). This two-fold division of responsibility can be traced back to the teaching of Jesus himself (see Extract 1).

1 "You shall have no other gods before me. You shall not make for yourself an idol . . ."

God made himself known to the Israelites by freeing them from the bondage of Egyptian slavery. After more than four hundred years they had been released by God's power alone. Because of this the Israelites were to worship no other gods but God and make no image of God in wood or stone.

This first commandment has enormous implications for all Christians. God is a constant, unchanging being who is always faithful, just and almighty, yet is merciful to those who believe. When this God reveals himself to a person they cannot respond by their own faith alone, since that is inadequate. God alone provides them with the capacity to love him in return. As Extract 1 shows, the first commandment calls all people to love God above everything, and everyone, else.

2 "You shall not misuse the name of the Lord your God."

This commandment calls for great respect to be shown to God's name. It use must be reserved for those occasions when a person is blessing, praising or glorifying God. Blasphemy, the sin of misusing God's name, is the ultimate betrayal of God. The CCC warns all believers of the words of St James, who condemned those 'who blaspheme that honourable name by which you are called' (James 2:7). Catholics are also forbidden to blaspheme against the Church of Christ, the saints including the Virgin Mary and all sacred things. Instead they should bear witness to God by confessing his name fearlessly in front of everyone.

3 "Remember the Sabbath Day by keeping it holy."

This commandment about keeping the Sabbath Day holy brings to mind two events:
- the creation of the world, when God worked for six days and then rested.
- the release of the Jews from slavery in Egypt – an event known as the Exodus.

God gave the Sabbath Day to the Jews as an unbreakable sign of his covenant (agreement) with them. The day was set aside for the people to use as a time of rest when everyone could praise God and be eternally grateful for his saving acts on their behalf.

Jesus respected the Sabbath laws but he also commented that 'the Sabbath was made for man and not man for the Sabbath' (Mark 2:27). For Christians there are no events as important as the passion, death and resurrection of Jesus. The resurrection, the beginning of a new creation, took place on a Sunday (the Lord's Day) so it was natural that this day should become special to the followers of Jesus. By the fourth century Christians were meeting for worship on the Sunday, the first day of the week, rather than on the Sabbath. Today Catholics should worship together each Sunday or keep the Sunday vigil (Saturday evening) in their parish communities. The Eucharist is at the very heart of Christian life and worship. Sharing the eucharistic celebration together is a public declaration that Catholics belong to Jesus and are part of his living community, the Church.

The Ten Commandments are prominently displayed in every Jewish synagogue. Do you think it would be helpful to have a reminder of them in every Catholic church?

WORK TO DO

1 a) Why did God demand that he alone should be worshipped?
  b) Why did God tell the Israelites that they should not make, or worship, any idols?

2 a) What is blasphemy?
  b) What is the link between blasphemy and the second commandment?
  c) Apart from God, who or what else does the CCC suggest that it is possible to blaspheme against?

3 a) What is the Sabbath Day?
  b) On which two events in Jewish history was the keeping of the Sabbath Day as a time of rest based?
  c) What do you think Jesus meant when he said: 'The Sabbath was made for man and not man for the Sabbath' (Mark 2:27)?
  d) Why did Sunday replace the Sabbath Day as the special day of worship for Christians?

DISCUSSION POINT

The CCC says that the Ten Commandments are 'grave obligations'. What do you think this means?

KEY WORDS

Eucharist
Moses
Sabbath Day
Sunday
Ten Commandments
Virgin Mary

1.3 THE TEN COMMANDMENTS (2)

The obligations to love God and to love our neighbour are closely linked. Jesus showed that very clearly (Matthew 22:37–40). The love that we are to show to our neighbour begins with our parents and then extends to those around us in society.

KEY QUESTION

What do the Ten Commandments teach us about our responsibilities to other people?

CONSULT

Exodus 20:12–17

Extract 1

Respect for parents derives from gratitude towards those who, by the gift of life, have brought their children into the world and enabled them to grow in stature, wisdom and grace.

CCC (2215)

4 "Honour your father and mother."

The duty to love begins with those to whom we owe the most – our parents. The commandment to honour them highlights the sacredness of the family, which God has placed at the heart of society. The family is a community of persons, each of whom is equal in dignity. It is:

- a living symbol of the three Persons in the Trinity
- a 'domestic church' – a community of faith and hope which is nourished by regular prayer and reading of the Scriptures.

Children must respect their parents for the gift of life which they have given to them. They must show this respect while they live under the same roof and maintain it after they have left home. They must meet the needs of their parents in sickness and old age, since the obligation to love them only ends when their parents die.

5 "Thou shall not murder."

This commandment teaches us to respect all human life since it is sacred. This is true from the moment of conception until a person dies. Since all human beings owe their continued existence to the goodness of God the premature ending of that life is a grave sin. The Roman Catholic Church opposes abortion, euthanasia, suicide and capital punishment because of this commandment.

6 and 9 "You shall not commit adultery . . . You shall not covet your neighbour's wife."

These two commandments forbidding the coveting of a neighbour's wife and adultery are closely linked. Our sexuality is a gift from God and, used properly, it helps us to love and cherish one another. To maintain it in the way God intended, the Catholic is called to live a chaste life – inside and outside marriage. This 'vocation' cannot be reconciled with such sexual activities as fornication, pornography, prostitution or homosexual behaviour. To help us avoid them God gives us guidance through the Church, the Holy Spirit, the Sacraments and prayer.

7 and 10 "You shall not steal . . . You shall not covet anything that belongs to your neighbour."

These commandments underline the importance of material possessions. The Catholic Church teaches that people have the right to their own private property and possessions. This was a right that Jesus recognised but he insisted that people should not become too strongly attached to their possessions (Matthew 6:25–34). A person's treasure in heaven is much more important than their possessions on earth (Matthew 6:19–24).

9 "You shall not give false testimony against your neighbour."

This commandment forbids us to misrepresent the truth. It demands that we live a life built on the truth, guarding against all forms of lying and hypocrisy. When we follow this commandment we are treating others justly, we are witnessing to the truth as we know it in Christ and we are making that truth known to others.

How do you think the children in this family could obey the fourth commandment?

WORK TO DO

1 One of the Ten Commandments is to 'honour our father and mother'.
   a) Explain one way in which people today can honour their parents.
   b) What promise is given in this commandment to those who fulfil its demands?

2 One of the Ten Commandments says that adultery is wrong.
   a) What is adultery?
   b) Give one reason why many people commit adultery today.
   c) How is this commandment linked with the one forbidding covetousness?

Extract 2

Human life is sacred because from its beginning it involves the creative action of God and it remains for ever in a special relationship with the Creator, who is its sole end. God alone is the Lord of life from its beginning until its end: no one can under any circumstances claim for himself the right directly to destroy an innocent human being.

CCC (2258)

DISCUSSION POINT

Jesus said that loving God and loving one's neighbours are the two great commandments. What do you think is the link between them?

KEY WORDS

Abortion
Adultery
Euthanasia
Fornication
Holy Spirit
Homosexuality
Sacrament
Suicide
Ten Commandments
Trinity
Vocation

1.4 THE BEATITUDES (1)

KEY QUESTION

Where did Jesus suggest that true happiness is to be found?

CONSULT

Matthew 5:3–6

Extract 1

How is it, then, that I seek you, Lord? Since in seeking you, my God, I seek a happy life, let me seek you so that my soul may live, for my body draws life from my soul and my soul draws life from you.

St Augustine

Extract 2

The Beatitudes depict the countenance of Jesus Christ and portray his charity. They express the vocation of the faithful associated with the glory of his Passion and Resurrection; they shed light on the actions and attitudes characteristic of the Christian life; they are the paradoxical promises that sustain hope in the midst of tribulations; they proclaim the blessings and rewards already secured, however dimly, for Christ's disciples; they have begun in the lives of the Virgin Mary and all the saints.

CCC (1717)

The natural human desire for happiness comes from God (see Extract 1). This desire draws us to worship the God who alone can give such happiness. The Ten Commandments (see 1.2 and 1.3), the teachings of the apostles in the New Testament and the teachings of Christ in the Sermon on the Mount (see 1.6 and 1.7) are all God-given to help us to find true happiness. The Beatitudes, the most important part of the Sermon on the Mount, encourage us to seek that happiness (beatitude) for which God has created us. The CCC underlines the importance of the Beatitudes for every Catholic (see Extract 2). In this unit we will look at the first four of the Beatitudes.

1 "Blessed are the poor in spirit, for theirs is the kingdom of heaven."

Jesus came to usher in God's kingdom (the kingdom of heaven) on earth by proclaiming his message of forgiveness to the poor and needy. Throughout his ministry Jesus associated with the outsiders, the downtrodden, the rejected and the poor. At no time did he suggest that it was good to be poor but simply that the attitudes associated with poverty – vulnerability and openness – are important spiritual qualities. Spiritual poverty leads to a humility in which we recognise that we are totally dependent on God. Being generous to others is a sign that we recognise this since, in giving to those in need, we are giving to God (Matthew 25:31–46). Those who accept their own poverty of spirit have begun to find the true source of happiness. God will give them a share in his kingdom.

2 "Blessed are those who mourn, for they will be comforted."

This Beatitude offers comfort to those who mourn the loss of a loved one. Its Jewish background reminds us that the Jews have a carefully constructed programme of mourning for those who are bereaved. By following this, everyone who mourns can come to experience the comfort which God alone offers. The Beatitude also refers to those who mourn for the world that God has made. God promises comfort for those who lament their own sins and those of others.

3 "Blessed are the meek for they will inherit the earth."

The meek or gentle are those who are unassuming, patient and tolerant. This is a virtue that Jesus showed throughout his life and death when he accepted, without complaint, everything that others did to him. God, too, shows this quality in all his dealings with us, sinful creatures that we are. When we recognise the dignity of God in others and share in all their weakness we, too, are fulfilling this Beatitude. Meek people are those who seek to solve the problems of others, without recrimination, in a spirit of gentle caring.

4 "Blessed are those who hunger and thirst for righteousness, for they will be filled."

'Hunger and thirst' is a phrase which vividly expresses an 'intense desire'. The same intense desire was expressed by St Augustine who said: 'Our hearts were made for you, O God, and they are restless until they rest in you'. In this Beatitude Jesus is praising those who realise that they have been created to praise God and that they can only be truly happy if they do so. Such people not only seek to do God's will wholly from the heart but also pray that his justice may be seen everywhere in the world. Unrighteousness in any form upsets them deeply.

Catholics know that human beings have been created to seek and know God. In seeking God's holiness and Christ's friendship they know that their own spiritual needs will be met. They appreciate the Eucharist and the other Sacraments as the God-given way for them to grow in holiness and righteousness. They know in their own lives the truth of the statement by St Thomas Aquinas that 'God alone satisfies'.

WORK TO DO

1 a) What message of Jesus ushered in God's kingdom?
   b) Which desirable qualities did Jesus suggest were most likely to be found in the poor?

2 a) Which two kinds of mourning did Jesus have in mind when he suggested that those who mourned would be comforted?
   b) How do you think that this Beatitude might offer comfort to people today?

3 a) What is meekness?
   b) Give two examples of how Jesus showed this quality in his own life.
   c) Give two examples of how people today might show the quality of meekness in their daily lives.

Why do you think that Jesus used small children more than once to teach his disciples about meekness and humility?

DISCUSSION POINT

What do you think are the most important spiritual qualities for a Christian to show in the modern world – and why?

KEY WORDS

Apostle
Beatitudes
Eucharist
New Testament
Sacrament
Saint
Sermon on the Mount
Ten Commandments
Virgin Mary

1.5 THE BEATITUDES (2)

KEY QUESTION

What do the Beatitudes say about the eternal happiness of all those who follow Jesus?

CONSULT

Matthew 5:7–12;
Luke 6:20–23

Extract 1

There we shall rest and see, we shall see and love, we shall love and praise. Behold what will be at the end without end. For what other end do we have, if not to reach the kingdom which has no end.

St Augustine, The City of God, *quoted in CCC (1720)*

Extract 2

The Decalogue [Ten Commandments], the Sermon on the Mount, and the apostolic catechesis (the teaching of the apostles) describe for us the paths that lead to the Kingdom of heaven. Sustained by the grace of the Holy Spirit, we tread them, step by step, by everyday acts. By the working of the Word of Christ, we slowly bear fruit in the Church to the glory of God.

CCC (1724)

The New Testament uses several expressions to help us to understand the happiness (beatitude) to which God calls all people. It speaks of:

- the coming of God's kingdom (Matthew 4:17)
- the vision of God (Matthew 5:8)
- entering into the joy of the Lord (Matthew 25:21–23)
- entering into God's rest (Hebrews 4:7–11)

We have been put into this world by God to know, love and serve him. True happiness leads us to share in the life of God on earth and the joys of eternal life in the world to come (see Extract 1). This is underlined in the remaining Beatitudes.

1 "Blessed are the merciful for they will be shown mercy."

In the Lord's Prayer (Matthew 6–12) a person asks God to forgive them because they have forgiven others. One depends on the other. No one can deserve or earn God's forgiveness. God forgives all who ask him and accepts them into his family as his adopted children. In return, each child of God is expected to extend love, mercy and forgiveness to others. By showing love and genuine concern to them we are showing that God is loving and merciful to all.

2 "Blessed are the pure in heart for they will see God."

The pure, or clean, in heart are those who have a single-minded commitment to God and his kingdom. This Beatitude forces us to face up to the priorities of life. Family, career and friends are all immensely important to us, and rightly so, but they are secondary in importance compared with our relationship with God. Each follower of Jesus is called to seek, and carry out, the will of God in their own life. To do this they must place the kingdom of God, and its demands, first.

3 "Blessed are the peacemakers for they will be called sons of God."

Love and peace are two personal hallmarks of the children of God. Christians will never knowingly seek, or cause, strife. They have a responsibility to struggle against conflict and disharmony wherever it is found. They do this when they help others to see that we all belong to a common brotherhood under God. Jesus was the supreme example of a peacemaker since he brought together God and man through his reconciling death on the cross. Each Christian is called to be an agent of God's peace in the world.

4 "Blessed are those who are persecuted because of righteousness, for theirs is the kingdom of heaven."

There is no greater sign of a person's commitment to God than their willingness to suffer for him. The supreme example again is Jesus. His agony in the Garden of Gethsemane, and on the cross of Calvary, shows the struggle involved in fully accepting God's will. If Jesus struggled to do this then it must be much more difficult for us. Yet this is the path that each Christian is called to tread. To be a Christian means being prepared to stand up for one's convictions, even if this means rejection, abuse or even martyrdom. The reward that Jesus promised those prepared to pay the ultimate price is nothing less than heaven – and the eternal happiness that it brings.

As the CCC emphasises, God put us into the world 'to know, to love and to serve him.' God's happiness enables us to share in his nature and eternal life. With this happiness we enter into the glory of Christ and into the joy that each member of the Trinity enjoys. In a real sense, we share the life of God.

How did Jesus show in his own life the qualities that he also expected his disciples to demonstrate?

WORK TO DO

1 How does the New Testament help us to understand the true happiness to which we are all called?

2 What kind of people are given the privilege of seeing God?

3 How is each Christian called to be the agent of God's peace – and what will be their reward?

4 a) Describe four things that the Beatitudes say about true peace.
   b) What rewards are offered to the person who enters into God's happiness in each case?

1.6 THE SERMON ON THE MOUNT (1)

KEY QUESTION

What does the Sermon on the Mount teach about the way that we should treat other people?

CONSULT

Matthew 5:21–6 and 38–48; 6:1–4; 7:1–6; 7:12

Extract 1

So in everything, do to others what you would have them do to you, for this sums up the Law and the Prophets.

'The Golden Rule', Matthew 7:12

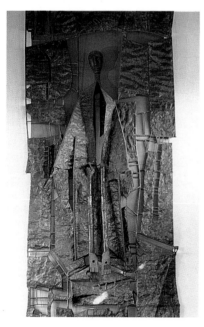

Do you think that the demands which Jesus laid down in the Sermon on the Mount are realistic or not?

The Sermon on the Mount is the name given to the collection of the teachings of Jesus found in chapters 5–7 of Matthew's Gospel. (A similar, but much briefer, collection is also found in Luke 6:17–49.) Matthew's collection brings together much of the teaching of Jesus on how his followers should behave and live. In particular, the material in the Sermon on the Mount gives clear advice about how the followers of Jesus should treat other people. Jesus often does this by taking a commandment from the Jewish Law (the Torah) and giving, by way of contrast, his own slant on the teaching. This teaching either contradicts, or deepens, the teaching of the Torah. Inevitably this caused great anguish to his Jewish listeners, for whom the Torah was God's greatest gift to the Jewish people and the foundation of their religious experience.

Anger (Matthew 5:21–26)

One of the Ten Commandments is 'Thou shalt not kill'. Jesus, though, went much further when he told his disciples: 'Anyone who is angry with his brother will be subjected to judgement' (5:22). No one can worship God properly while they are involved in a dispute or argument with someone else. The dispute must be settled first and then God will be able to accept the worship they are offering.

Revenge (Matthew 5:38–42)

Jesus quoted a law from the Torah (Exodus 21:24) that was intended to keep revenge within limits. The law said: 'An eye for an eye and a tooth for a tooth'. Jesus ruled this out and dismissed the idea that revenge could be acceptable in any situation. He told his followers: 'If someone strikes you on the right cheek, turn to him the other also' (Matthew 5:39). The followers of Jesus were not to retaliate even if someone took them to court or if a Roman soldier forced them to carry his pack. Jesus told his followers that they should be prepared to give their possessions away to those who asked for them.

Love your enemies (Matthew 5:43–48)

The Torah taught Jewish people to love their neighbours (Leviticus 19:18) and some understood this to refer only to their fellow Jews. Those who want to belong to God's kingdom, however, must go much further than this. The followers of Jesus are told to: 'Love your enemies and pray for those who persecute you' (Matthew 5:42). They must aim for the highest possible goal even if they do not reach it: 'Be perfect, therefore, as your heavenly Father is perfect' (Matthew 5:48).

Judging others (Matthew 7:1–6)

Jesus taught that his followers should not judge the attitudes or actions of others. No one is good enough to judge someone else. The judgement of others must be left with God.

The Golden Rule (Matthew 7:12)

Jesus gave to his followers a rule (often called the 'Golden Rule') which, he said, summed up all that was found in the Torah and the Prophets (see Extract 1). The Jewish Scriptures were divided into three parts – the Torah, the Prophets and the Writings – and the first two of these were the most important. Jesus was spelling out all that was essential in Christian ethical teaching by summing up the Christian law of love. The followers of Jesus should treat others in the way that they would like others to treat them. The same teaching also sums up perfectly the ethical and moral teaching of the Roman Catholic Church.

WORK TO DO

1 List three teachings from the Sermon on the Mount about how we should treat other people.

2 a) Give two examples from the Sermon on the Mount of Jesus suggesting that his teaching goes beyond that found in the Jewish Scriptures.
   b) Explain what Jesus was concerned for his listeners to learn from these two examples.

3 a) What is the 'Golden Rule'?
   b) What did Jesus say was summed up by the Golden Rule?
   c) What lesson should followers of Jesus learn from the Golden Rule?

This group is meeting together during Lent to study the Bible. Why do you think that the Sermon on the Mount would be a good part of the Bible to study at this time?

Extract 2

The entire Law of the Gospel is contained in the 'new commandment' of Jesus, to love one another as he has loved us.

CCC (1970)

Extract 3

Christian prayer extends to the forgiveness of enemies, transfiguring the disciple by configuring him to his Master. Forgiveness is a high-point of Christian prayer; only hearts attuned to God's compassion can receive the gift of prayer. Forgiveness also bears witness that, in our world, love is stronger than sin.

CCC (2844)

DISCUSSION POINT

How practical do you think it is to put Jesus' teaching about not retaliating when threatened into practice today?

KEY WORDS

Prophets
Sermon on the Mount
Ten Commandments
Torah
Writings

1.7 THE SERMON ON THE MOUNT (2)

KEY QUESTION

What does the Sermon on the Mount say about marriage, divorce and prayer?

CONSULT

Matthew 5:27–32;
6:5–15

Extract 1

You have heard that it was said, 'Do not commit adultery'. But I tell you that anyone who looks at a woman lustfully has already committed adultery with her in his heart.

Matthew 5:27,28

Why did Jesus suggest that the best place for a person to pray was in the silence of their own room?

In addition to the teaching in the Sermon on the Mount on how we should treat other people (see 1.6), two other themes dominate. Jesus gave clear teaching about:
- Adultery and divorce
- Prayer.

Adultery

As we saw in 1.3, the sixth commandment forbids adultery. Once again, Jesus went beyond the surface meaning of the commandment to its heart. His teaching made greater demands on his followers than the Jewish law did (see Extract 1). To be true to his teaching, his followers must not even want to commit adultery. Sexual attraction is a natural part of our human personality and Jesus was not saying that that in itself was wrong. He was saying that people should not deliberately think about, and dwell upon, any desire which might lead them to seek sex with someone to whom they are not married.

Jesus gave a startling piece of advice (Matthew 5:27–35) to underline the seriousness of what he was saying. He was not, of course, suggesting that a person who is contemplating adultery should really gouge out an eye or cut off a hand. He wanted people to see that living in God's kingdom, with all its demands, is the most important thing in life. No sacrifice is too great to make in order to enter that kingdom.

Divorce

Jesus referred his listeners back to the old Jewish law on divorce: 'Anyone who divorces his wife must give her a certificate of divorce' (Deuteronomy 24:1–4). The Torah allowed a man to divorce his wife if she was guilty of 'some shameful conduct', which for many rabbis could only mean adultery. Others, though, interpreted the law more liberally. This meant that, in the time of Jesus, a Jewish man could easily obtain a divorce although divorce was not available to women. In the Sermon on the Mount Jesus allows divorce for adultery (see Extract 2), although in Mark 10:11–12 and Luke 16:18 he seems to rule out divorce altogether. It is likely that Mark and Luke retain an earlier reading of the teaching of Jesus which had been 'softened' somewhat by the time that Matthew wrote his Gospel in around 80 CE.

Prayer

The Sermon on the Mount contains some of the most important teaching in the Gospels about prayer and fasting (going without food for a religious reason). In Matthew 6:5–18 Jesus tells his followers that they should not be interested in receiving the praise or approval of others when they pray – they should simply concentrate their hearts and minds on God. The best place to pray is in the silence of one's own room, alone with God. The only acceptable prayers are those which simply speak to God from the heart, not those which use elaborate phrases or words.

To help his followers to put these simple principles into practice when they pray, Jesus gave to his disciples the model prayer – the Lord's Prayer or the 'Our Father' (Pater Noster). Notice that, after praising God and asking that his kingdom will be built on earth, the prayer brings the basic needs of each day to God: 'Give us today our daily bread' (Matthew 6:11). The important spiritual message that the Christian life should be lived day by day, trusting in God, is taken up later in the Sermon (Matthew 6:25–34). Then come the important lines in the prayer about forgiveness – no matter how badly other people have hurt us we have a duty to forgive them before we can expect God to forgive our sins. The Lord's Prayer finishes with the request that God will keep us safe from temptation – and the Evil One (Satan).

WORK TO DO

1 What did Jesus say about adultery in the Sermon on the Mount?

2 a) What did the Jewish law teach about divorce?
   b) What did Jesus teach about divorce in the Sermon on the Mount?

3 The Lord's Prayer says something very important about forgiveness. What is it?

4 What did Jesus say about prayer in the Sermon on the Mount?

5 Read Matthew 5:38–42 and 6:12. How do you think that the teaching of Jesus might influence a Christian's attitude to punishment today?

This person is using a yad to follow a passage in the Hebrew Scriptures so that they do not touch the Holy Scriptures. What did Jesus say about the importance of these Scriptures in Matthew 5:17–20?

Extract 2

I tell you that anyone who divorces his wife, except for marital unfaithfulness, causes her to become an adulteress, and anyone who marries the divorced woman commits adultery.

Matthew 5:32

Extract 3

Adultery is an injustice. He who commits adultery fails in his commitment. He does injury to the sign of the covenant which the marriage bond is, transgresses the rights of the other spouse and undermines the institution of marriage by breaking the contract on which it is based.

CCC (2381)

DISCUSSION POINT

Why do you think the Church may have softened the teaching of Jesus on divorce by the time that Matthew wrote his Gospel?

KEY WORDS

Adultery
Gospel
Lord's Prayer
Rabbi
Satan
Sermon on the Mount
Torah

CHRISTIAN DISCIPLESHIP

2.1 DISCIPLESHIP

Jesus did not come to call people to start, or join, a new religion. During less than three years of public ministry he told people about the closeness of God's kingdom, calling those who listened, and responded, to his message to a life of service and discipleship. This call to discipleship was at the very heart of his message to the people.

KEY QUESTION

What kind of life did Jesus call his followers to live as his disciples?

CONSULT

Mark 10:17–31

Discipleship

The word 'disciple' is found more than 250 times in the New Testament, mostly in the Gospels and the Acts of the Apostles. The verb 'to follow' appears more than 70 times. A Christian disciple is someone who follows the example and teachings of Jesus of Nazareth. The people who followed religious leaders before Jesus attached themselves to the one whose teaching inspired them. However, the Gospels make it clear that Jesus chose his disciples, as you will see in 2.2, Simon, Andrew and Matthew were among those hand-picked and given the opportunity to respond to the call of Jesus (Mark 1:17; 2:14).

Jesus chose some surprising people to be his followers. Amongst those he invited to follow him were the tax collectors and sinners that he was strongly criticised for associating with (Mark 2:16). Although women were not chosen to be amongst his twelve disciples there were many females in the wider circle of followers who shared their lives with him (Luke 8:2).

Being called by Jesus to be a disciple involved a radical change of heart, a change which the Gospel writers often symbolised as leaving behind everything. The story of the rich young ruler who approached Jesus illustrates this perfectly. To this young man, who had kept all of the Jewish commandments from his youth, Jesus said, 'One thing you lack. Go, sell everything you have and give to the poor, and you will have treasure in heaven. Then come, follow me.' (Mark 10:21). In the Gospels those who followed Jesus 'left everything' (Luke 5:11), including work (Mark 2:14), family and children (Luke 14:26). For some, being a disciple even included **celibacy**, which they embraced for the sake of God and his kingdom (Matthew 19:11,12).

Being a disciple meant sharing in the ministry of Jesus. Jesus sent the disciples out to teach others and act in his name by healing the sick, casting out demons and telling everyone that the kingdom of God had arrived (Mark 6:7–13). Jesus warned them that they would be rejected and lose the support of their families (Matthew 10:1–42). Despite this, they were still to share all they had with others (Luke 6:30) by serving them (Mark 9:35). Their lives were to be lived with sacrificial love – an ideal of discipleship which is perfectly expressed in Extract 1.

Extract 1

> This is my commandment: love one another as I love you. No one has greater love than this, to lay down one's life for one's friends.

John 15:12–13

Extract 2

> If anyone would come after me, he must deny himself and take up his cross and follow me. For whoever wants to save his life will lose it, but whoever loses his life for me and for the gospel will save it.

Mark 8:34,35

What do you think it means for each person in this congregation to be a disciple of Jesus today?

After Easter

After the first Easter the disciples began to understand that following Jesus might involve them paying the ultimate price – giving their own life. Mark united the idea of following Jesus with martyrdom when he spoke of taking up one's cross and being willing to give up one's life for the Gospel (see Extract 2). The early Church saw martyrdom as the highest expression of discipleship.

Discipleship in the Gospels means making a personal, and often very costly, decision that will affect every dimension of life. It dictates all human and family relationships, shapes personal attitudes to property and wealth, gives a new order of priorities and a new meaning to love. It gives a whole new meaning to personal fulfilment and calls the person to enter into the deeper meaning of Christ's paschal mystery – the passage from life to death and back to life again. At its heart is what the Catholic tradition has long called the *imitatio Christi*, the imitation of Christ.

WORK TO DO

1 What was different about the life of discipleship which Jesus called his followers to adopt?

2 Why do you think that Jesus hand-picked his closest disciples rather than waiting for people to attach themselves to him – as other religious leaders did at the time?

3 What was involved for those who were called by Jesus to be his disciples?

4 'Good teacher, what must I do to inherit eternal life?' Give an account of the meeting of Jesus with the rich young man who asked this question and describe the answer that Jesus gave to it.

DISCUSSION POINT

What do you think is involved in being a disciple of Jesus as the Church moves into the twenty-first century?

KEY WORDS

Acts of the Apostles
Celibacy
Easter
Gospel
New Testament
Paschal Mystery

2.2 THE CALL AND MISSION OF THE DISCIPLES

KEY QUESTION

What was distinctive about the mission that Jesus gave to his disciples, both during his time with them and afterwards?

CONSULT

Mark 3:13–19 and 6:7–13;
Matthew 28:16–20

Extract 1

The transmission of the Christian faith consists primarily in proclaiming Jesus Christ in order to lead others to faith in him. From the beginning, the first disciples burned with the desire to proclaim Christ: 'We cannot but speak of what we have seen and heard'. And they invite people of every era to enter into the joy of their communion with Christ.

CCC (425)

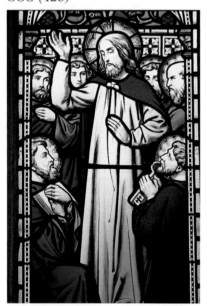

What was unusual about the way that the disciples of Jesus were chosen?

The disciples of Jesus played an important part in his life and ministry although only a handful of them figure prominently in the Gospel story. Many remained largely anonymous after the Gospel writers tell us that they were chosen by Jesus to be his closest companions and confidants.

Choosing the Twelve

Jesus broke with the convention of the time by choosing his own disciples (see 2.1). The Gospels tell us how Simon and Andrew (Mark 1:14–18), James and John (Mark 1:19,20), Philip and Nathaniel (John 1:43–51), Levi, also known as Matthew (Mark 2:13–17) and two unnamed disciples (John 1:35–39) were called by Jesus. A little later Jesus formalised the list of twelve disciples by calling them out from a much larger group of followers (Mark 3:13–19). Mark called this small group 'apostles' (those who are sent) although this title only seems to have been formally adopted to describe the group after the Day of Pentecost when they received the Holy Spirit (Acts 2:1–11).

Sending the disciples out

Mark tells us that Jesus chose his disciples for two reasons: that he 'might be with them' and that 'he might send them out to preach and to have authority to drive out demons' (Mark 3:14,15). These last two elements are closely connected – the salvation that Jesus brings involves the defeat of Satan and his demons. Later, Jesus sent the Twelve out on a mission. They were to travel from village to village, preaching the good news that the kingdom of God had come. Jesus had been preparing them for this time since he had called them with the promise 'I will make you fishers of men' (Mark 1:17). The instructions that Jesus gave to his disciples (Mark 6:6–13) show the great urgency with which they were to approach their mission:

- They were to take nothing with them for the journey except a staff – no bread, no bag, no money in their belts. They were to wear sandals but were not to carry an extra tunic.
- They were to stay in the same house while in a village. If they were not welcomed by any village then they were to shake the dust of that village off their feet and move on to the next one.

The word used here for 'sending' carries with it the idea of an official representation; the message and deeds of the disciples were to be an extension of those of Jesus himself. He sent them out 'two by two', apparently a Jewish custom, so that the truthfulness of their testimony to Jesus could be established 'on the testimony of two or three witnesses' (Deuteronomy 17:6).

The Great Commission

The Great Commission (Matthew 28:16–20) contains the last words of Jesus spoken on earth and it was given to the eleven disciples who remained after Jesus rose from the dead. Jesus began by stating that 'All authority in heaven and on earth has been given to me.' In the light of that authority the disciples, and all subsequent followers, were to:

- go into the world and make disciples from all nations on the earth.
- baptise all those who believed, in the name of God the Father, God the Son and God the Holy Spirit.
- teach new disciples to do everything that Jesus had told them.

For the past two thousand years this Commission has laid a heavy responsibility on the Church. There have been many – priests, religious and lay people – who have heard the call of Christ to carry the Gospel to the ends of the earth. Many of these have paid the ultimate price and lost their lives for the sake of the Gospel. All of them, though, have been faithful to the two-fold responsibility to preach the Good News of the Gospel and to baptise those who believe. This underlines the importance of the sacrament of baptism in the ministry of the Church.

WORK TO DO

1 Read the passage describing the Great Commission of Jesus to his disciples.
   a) Which Sacrament does the passage encourage?
   b) Jesus told his disciples to go to people everywhere and make disciples. How have some Christians throughout history shown their willingness to spend the whole of their lives doing this?
   c) What did Jesus say to his disciples which encouraged them to be involved in spreading the Gospel?

2 When Jesus sent out his disciples to preach and heal, what conditions did he lay down for them and why?

DISCUSSION POINT

How is the Church today trying to carry out the responsibility of the Great Commission to spread the Christian message? How successful do you think it is being?

KEY WORDS

Apostle
Baptism
Day of Pentecost
Disciple
Holy Spirit
Priest
Sacrament
Satan

Extract 2

That which was from the beginning, which we have heard, which we have seen with our eyes, which we have looked upon and touched with our hands, concerning the word of life – the life was made manifest, and we saw it, and testify to it, and proclaim to you the eternal life which was with the Father and was made manifest to us – that which we have seen and heard we also proclaim to you, so that you may have fellowship with us, and our fellowship is with the Father and with his Son Jesus Christ. And we are writing this that our joy may be complete.

1 John 1:1–4, quoted in CCC (425)

Jesus had many female followers. Why do you think that he did not choose any of them to be disciples?

2.3 THE COST OF DISCIPLESHIP

KEY QUESTION

What did Jesus expect of all those who responded to his challenge to become disciples?

CONSULT

Matthew 16:24;
Luke 14:28–32;
Matthew 8:21–22

Extract 1

As they were walking along the road a man said to him, 'I will follow you wherever you go.' Jesus replied, 'Foxes have holes and birds of the air have nests, but the Son of Man has nowhere to lay his head.'

He said to another man, 'Follow me.' But the man replied, 'Lord, first let me go and bury my father.' Jesus said to him, 'Let the dead bury their own dead but you go and proclaim the kingdom of God.'

Still another said, 'I will follow you, Lord; but first let me go back and say goodbye to my family.' Jesus replied, 'No one who puts his hands to the plough and looks back is fit for service in the kingdom of God.'

Luke 10:57–62

We have already discovered that discipleship was one of the central themes in the teaching of Jesus. Jesus came primarily to bring God's kingdom and to invite men and women to enter into it as his disciples. At the very beginning of his ministry Mark tells us that Jesus went into Galilee 'proclaiming the good news of God' and telling the people that 'The time has come. The Kingdom of God is near. Repent and believe the good news.' (1:14).

Making the commitment

In one sense, becoming a disciple of Jesus was easy. The kingdom of God was open to everyone who recognised their need and responded to the message of Jesus with faith. Many social outcasts – Roman soldiers, tax collectors, prostitutes and lepers – responded and were welcomed by God into the kingdom. Yet in another sense Jesus did not make it easy for people to become disciples. He made it clear that the cost could be immense. Turning to the crowds following him on one occasion he told them: 'If anyone comes to me and does not hate his father and mother, his wife and children, his brothers and sisters – yes, even his own life – he cannot be my disciple.' (Luke 14:26,27). To underline this he told people the following two parables:

a) When a person wants to build a tower on his land he first sits down and counts the cost carefully. If he doesn't he might lay the foundations and then not have enough money to complete the project. As a result everyone will ridicule him (Luke 14:28–30).

b) One king is about to declare war on another. Before he does so, surely he will wonder how, with 10,000 soldiers at his disposal, he can hope to defeat his enemy who can call on 20,000 troops.

Both the man building the tower and the king going to war need to commit themselves totally to the enterprise – otherwise they cannot hope to succeed. So, too, the person thinking of following Jesus must be prepared to make a total commitment – 'In the same way, any of you who does not give up everything he has cannot be my disciple' (Luke 14:33).

Counting the cost

Jesus spelt out the cost of following him in clear terms. He said that any would-be disciple must be prepared to:

- deny their own self-interests and desires. On many occasions Jesus told his disciples that they must deny themselves, take up their cross and follow him (see Matthew 16:24, for example). Denying oneself means setting aside one's own legitimate feelings and interests so that the needs of others can be met.
- place Jesus, first, before family and loved ones. We learn nothing from the Gospels about the families of the disciples although we have reason to believe that Peter, and some of the others, were married. As Extract 1 shows, Jesus made it clear to three potential disciples that he must come before all other commitments.

- face possible suffering and death. This was a very real possibility in the time of Jesus, and many who spent much time with Jesus, including Peter and James, ended up as martyrs. Jesus had promised them both suffering – 'If they persecuted me, they will persecute you also' (John 15:20) – and possible death – 'Whoever finds his life will lose it and whoever loses his life for my sake will find it' (Matthew 10:39). Quite often, Jesus said two opposing things in the same sentence, so that people would be jolted into grasping the depth of what he was trying to say. On one occasion, he was trying to show his disciples the truth that the Christian Gospel and God's kingdom were to be built on the blood of those who laid down their lives for their Saviour willingly. He told them that a seed could only grow into a tree if it fell into the ground and died first. He then said to them: 'The man who loves his life will lose it, while the man who hates his life in this life will keep it for eternal life' (John 12:25). This is the ultimate sacrifice that God can call any disciple to make.

WORK TO DO

1 St Rose of Lima said: 'Apart from the cross there is no other ladder by which we may get to heaven.' What do you think she meant?

2 What message stood at the centre of the teaching of Jesus?

3 Clearly Jesus was not expecting new disciples actually to 'hate' those who were nearest and dearest to them. Why, then, do you think he said that very thing?

Extract 2

The cross is the unique sacrifice of Christ, the 'one mediator between God and men'. But because in his incarnate divine person he has in some way united himself to every man, 'the possibility of being made partners, in a way known to God, in the paschal mystery' is offered to all men.

CCC (618)

DISCUSSION POINT

What do you think is likely to be the real cost of following Jesus for most people today?

KEY WORDS

Gospel
Paschal Mystery
Peter

Peter was put to death by the Roman Emperor Nero in 64 CE. Why do you think that martyrs were so highly regarded in the early Church?

The figure in the main panel of this window is Maximilian Kolbe, a Catholic priest put to death in the Second World War. Find out the background to his martyrdom.

2.4 THE KINGDOM OF GOD

KEY QUESTION

What did Jesus mean when he spoke to his disciples and others about the

CONSULT

Mark 1:14,15;
Luke 6:20–23 and
12:8,9

Extract 1

Jesus said [to his disciples]: 'Let the little children come to me, and do not hinder them, for the kingdom of God belongs to such as these. I tell you the truth, anyone who will not receive the kingdom of God like a little child will never enter it.'

Mark 10:14,15

Jesus said 'Anyone who will not receive the kingdom of God like a little child will not enter it.' What do you think he meant?

Without any question his baptism by John the Baptist was a turning-point in the life of Jesus, since it was followed by a theophany, that is, an encounter with God. As he saw the heavens above him open after he was baptised, Jesus was anointed by the Holy Spirit and proclaimed to be God's Son. Luke tells us that this encounter took place while Jesus 'was praying' (3:1) and the three Synoptic Gospels agree that he withdrew afterwards to spend time in the desert fasting and praying. Mark records the first public words of Jesus, in which he summed up the message that was to dominate the rest of his life: 'The right time has come . . . and the kingdom of God is near. Turn away (repent) your sins and believe the Good News.' (Mark 1:14).

The kingdom of God

The idea that dominated the preaching and teaching of Jesus was 'the kingdom of God', and he left the people in little doubt that this kingdom, or rule, was very close to them (Mark 1:15). Although this phrase has its roots in the Old Testament it is only seriously used in the Gospels. Jesus did not really explain what he understood by it, preferring instead to illustrate different aspects of it through many of his parables. In those parables the kingdom of God emerges as the present, and future, reign of God in the world:

- **The kingdom of God is here**   Jesus came to bring in God's kingdom through his preaching, parables, miracles, exorcisms, forgiveness of sins and by his 'table-teaching'. After driving a demon out of a person unable to speak, Jesus replied to those who criticised him for eating with social outcasts: 'But if it is by the finger of God that I drive out demons, then the kingdom of God has come upon you.' (Luke 11:20). The meals ('table-teaching') that Jesus had with sinners and others considered to be outside the Law show that God's kingdom is inclusive – no one is excluded. The parables of the kingdom (see 2.5) bring out both the present and the future dimensions of God's kingdom but they underline, above all else, that God is found amongst us. God's saving power is to be found as we reach out with compassion to others, just as Jesus did. Yet we must still wait patiently for the fulness of our salvation.

- **The kingdom of God is still to come**   The future dimension of God's kingdom is very clear in the teaching of Jesus. In the Lord's Prayer (the 'Our Father') Jesus taught his disciples to pray for the coming of God's kingdom, which had not yet arrived (Matthew 6:10). The Beatitudes promise future comfort and joy in God's kingdom for those who are now poor and hungry (Matthew 5:3–12). The future dimensions of God's reign are brought out in the Gospel sayings about the Son of Man, Jesus, coming to reign in glory and power (Luke 12:8,9).

Entering God's kingdom

Though all are invited to enter God's kingdom Jesus made it clear that, in the end, it is a matter of personal decision. To enter the kingdom each person must become like a little child (see Extract 1) and be converted after repenting of their sins (Mark 1:15). Through this they discover a life of discipleship in the service of God, who teaches them to love others with a self-sacrificial devotion which goes way beyond self-interest (Matthew 5:38–48). The Beatitudes, which are at the centre of the teaching of Jesus (see 1.4 and 1.5) describe those who will find deep fulfilment in God's kingdom. Ultimately, entrance into the kingdom is dependent on the way that we treat others, especially the poor and the unfortunate in society (Matthew 25:34–46). As you will see in Extract 2, the CCC underlines this very strongly.

WORK TO DO

1 a) What do you understand by the 'kingdom of God'?
  b) How important was the concept of the kingdom of God in the teaching of Jesus?

2 Write notes on the kingdom of God bearing in mind:
  a) its present aspect
  b) its future aspect.

3 How did Jesus bring in God's kingdom?

4 What did the frequent contact of Jesus with the social outcasts of his time show about the kingdom of God?

Women and children were two of the most vulnerable groups in the time of Jesus. Why do you think he often chose to direct his message about God's kingdom to them?

Extract 2

The kingdom belongs to the poor and lowly, which means those who have accepted it with humble hearts. Jesus is sent to 'preach good news to the poor', he declares them blessed, for 'theirs is the kingdom of heaven'. To them – the 'little ones' – the Father is pleased to reveal what remains hidden from the wise and learned. Jesus shares the life of the poor, from the cradle to the cross; he experiences hunger, thirst and privation. Jesus identifies himself with the poor of every kind and makes active love toward them the condition for entering his kingdom.

CCC (544)

DISCUSSION POINT

Why do you think that Jesus did not explain directly what he understood by the kingdom of God but preferred instead to give glimpses of it through his parables?

KEY WORDS

Beatitudes
Gospel
Holy Spirit
John the Baptist
Lord's Prayer
Old Testament
Son of Man
Synoptic Gospels

2.5 PARABLES OF GOD'S KINGDOM

There are 40 different parables recorded in the three Synoptic Gospels and the majority of these are concerned with the kingdom of God. Each of them provides us with a snapshot of some aspect of that kingdom. In this section we will look at just four of them.

KEY QUESTION

What do we learn from the parables of Jesus about the nature of God's kingdom?

CONSULT

Mark 4:1–20 and 30–32; Matthew 13:24–30 and 47–50

1 The parable of the sower (Mark 4:1–20)

This story is unusual as it is followed, almost directly, by an interpretation (see the parable of the weeds below). Usually Jesus told a parable and then left his listeners to work out its meaning for themselves. From this interpretation, which probably came from the early Church and not from Jesus himself, we find out about the progress of God's kingdom amongst different groups of people. In Palestine the sowing of seed came before the ploughing of the ground and so some parts of the field did not offer suitable conditions for seed to grow:

- some seed fell on the pathway allowing the birds to gobble it up (4:3)
- some fell on ground where the soil was thin and the sun quickly scorched it (4:5)
- some fell among thorn bushes which choked the seed (4:7).

Each point in the story, Mark explains, carries its own meaning. The sower, Jesus, and those disciples who follow after him sow God's message about his kingdom. Those who listen to the message fall into different categories. There are those who are so 'hard' that the message does not penetrate at all. As soon as they hear it the 'Evil One', Satan, snatches the message away. Some are like rocky ground – they are pleased to hear the message but they do not retain it for long. Others are like the thorn bushes because, when they hear the message, they allow the cares of this world or the love of money to kill it. Some people, though, are like fertile ground which receives and nourishes the words of Jesus. They become committed followers of Jesus and so are part of God's kingdom.

2 The parable of the mustard seed (Mark 4:30–32)

In the time of Jesus the mustard seed was proverbial for its smallness but the tiny seed grows into a huge, tree-like shrub. The main point of this brief parable (see Extract 1) is that the kingdom of God has insignificant and small beginnings but the day will come when it will be large and powerful. We should not judge the significance of God's kingdom by the size of its beginnings. The day has not yet arrived when the full extent of God's kingdom will be revealed.

Extract 1

He told them another parable: 'The kingdom of heaven is like a mustard seed, which a man took and planted in his field. Though it is the smallest of your seeds, yet when it grows, it is the largest of the garden plants and becomes a tree, so that the birds of the air come and perch in its branches.'

He told them still another parable: 'The kingdom of heaven [God] is like yeast that a woman took and mixed into a large amount of flour until it worked all through the dough.'

Matthew 13:31–33

3 The parable of the weeds (Matthew 13:24–30)

The parable of the sower, described above, shows that the kingdom will gather in many people, despite hard hearts and competing pressures. This parable shows that God's kingdom will continue to grow alongside everything that would destroy it, until the final harvest. The destructive weeds, as we learn from Matthew 13:36–43, are sown by the 'Evil One' and they continue to grow alongside the seeds that have been sown by the Son of Man, Jesus. It is only when the end of the age arrives that the Son of Man will harvest the good crop and throw the weeds into the fires of judgement. In this world, though, the two will continue to grow side by side.

4 The parable of the net (Matthew 13:47–52)

This parable follows on from the story of the weeds. There is a difference, though. The parable of the weeds concentrates on the long time when the good seeds and the weeds grow side by side. The parable of the net describes the situation which exists at the time when the Last Judgement takes place. The kingdom of God contains both good and bad fish, with the sorting out taking place after the final sweep of the net.

WORK TO DO

1 Explain what you have learned about the kingdom of God from two of the parables that Jesus told to illustrate this theme.

2 Explain what Christians can learn from the parable of the sower.
   a) Give two ways in which Catholics believe that they can listen to what Jesus has to say.
   b) Some people in the parable did not listen to Jesus. Suggest one reason why people today may not be interested in the teaching of Jesus.

Extract 2

Jesus spoke all these things to the crowds in parables; he did not say anything to them without using a parable. So was fulfilled what was spoken through the prophet: 'I will open my mouth in parables, I will utter things hidden since the creation of the world.'

Matthew 13:34–35

DISCUSSION POINT

Jesus suggested that different things happen to the seed that falls on rocky places and the seed that falls amongst thorns. What do you think are the modern equivalents which prevent the message about God's kingdom taking root and growing in many people today?

KEY WORDS

Parable
Satan
Son of Man
Synoptic Gospel

Why do you think that so many people do not respond to the challenge of Jesus?

③ POVERTY AND JUSTICE

3.1 RICH AND POOR COUNTRIES

KEY QUESTION

What do we mean when we speak of the north/south or rich/poor divide?

As far as wealth and poverty are concerned the world today can broadly be divided into two areas:

1 The Northern or Developed world, ('First World') This consists of countries which have a high standard of living and includes North America, Western Europe including Britain, and Australasia. These countries have only 25 per cent of the world's population (about 1,500 million people) but they consume 75 per cent of the world's wealth.

2 The Southern or Developing world, ('Third World') These are countries which have a much lower standard of living. Although 75 per cent of the world's population live in the Developing World it only has 25 per cent of the world's resources to sustain it. Some developing countries are very poor (Sudan, Somalia and Bangladesh, for example) whilst others (such as Peru and Bolivia) are less so.

Extract 1

Many hundreds of millions of people are preoccupied solely with survival and elementary needs. For them work is frequently not available or, when it is, pay is very low and conditions are often barely tolerable. Homes are constructed of permeable [non-waterproof] materials and have neither piped water nor sanitation. Electricity is a luxury ... Primary schools, where they exist, may be free and not too far away but children are needed for work and cannot easily be spared for schooling ... Flood, drought or disease affecting people or livestock can easily destroy livelihoods without hope of compensation.

Brandt Report

The developed and developing worlds

Many people in the world are 'poor' but it is very important to distinguish between 'absolute poverty' and 'relative poverty'. Some parts of Britain are poor compared with other parts of the country. This is called relative poverty. It is 'relative' to other people in Britain but even the poorest parts of Britain are rich compared to many developing countries. Many people in developing countries live in absolute poverty. This means that they are very poor whatever standard is applied to their lifestyle. Such absolute poverty can be measured by using the following standards:

- **a high level of malnutrition.** In the world's poorest countries up to 75 per cent of the population try to make a living out of agriculture, compared with just 5 per cent in Britain. This is largely 'subsistence farming' with people desperately hoping to grow enough to meet their own needs. They have little left over to sell and no money to buy those things that they cannot grow.
- **a low level of literacy and education.** There is a direct link between the level of poverty and the level of literacy in poor countries. People who are illiterate (about 850 million throughout the world) can find no way out of the poverty trap.
- **a high level of illness and disease.** If children living in developing countries survive the perils of childbirth, they find as they grow up that their living conditions leave them vulnerable to all kinds of illness and disease. At least 25 per cent of the world's population, for instance, do not have access to clean water.
- **a high rate of infant mortality.** Children are most vulnerable in the first year of their lives. Fifteen million children under

the age of five die of malnutrition each year. Malnourished mothers are unable to provide milk for their underfed babies and so the cycle of poverty continues unabated.

- **a low life expectancy.** In the United Kingdom men can reasonably hope to reach the age of 71 and women 76. In many developing countries the life expectancy for both men and women is little more than 45.

Short and long-term aid

Most countries accept that they need to give or receive aid. This aid can come in the form of food, shelter, medical personnel and supplies, or loans of money.

Short-term aid is provided when a natural disaster hits a poor country – as it frequently does in the form of earthquakes, floods, typhoons or other extreme weather. Other countries need to act very quickly to get the aid to the places where it is needed and such aid often makes a great difference to people's chances of surviving the disaster.

Long-term aid, however, is different. Its aim is to help poorer countries to overcome underlying problems. Examples include providing help to build hospitals and schools, advice to improve the productivity of the soil, or assistance in constructing irrigation systems to take water to remote areas. Usually, unfortunately, such aid comes with strings attached (such as an agreement by the poorer country to buy goods from the donor country), which means the donor country benefits as well as the country receiving the help. Britain donates only about 0.3 per cent of its wealth each year to poorer countries.

WORK TO DO

1 Explain the difference between short-term and long-term aid.

2 Describe three differences between countries in the developed world and those in the developing world.

3 What is the difference between relative poverty and absolute poverty?

Why are babies and the very young so vulnerable to poverty?

DISCUSSION POINT

Clearly the world's wealth is very unfairly distributed. Should the world's wealthy countries be prepared to share much of their wealth with those countries which have very little?

What is meant by subsistence farming?

3.2 WORLD HUNGER

KEY QUESTION

What is the truth about hunger and malnutrition in the world today?

Extract 1

a) There are 3500 calories per kilo of grain so a tonne of grain supplies an average of 3.5 million calories.

b) About 2300 calories a day is adequate for proper nutrition.

c) At 2300 calories a day for 365 days a person needs 839,500 calories a year. This means that a tonne of grain would feed four people for a year.

d) A million tonnes would feed more than 4 million people. Five million tonnes would feed 20 million people – the number that die from malnutrition each year.

Susan George, Economist

The simple statistics about hunger in the world today are staggering. Each year it is thought that more than 20 million people die from malnutrition and that 50 per cent of these people have not reached their fifth birthday. Many more people die from hunger (malnutrition) and related illnesses than from any other cause, including war. Malnutrition kills:

- 1 person every 1.5 seconds
- 38 people every minute
- 55,000 people every day.

The paradox of hunger

World hunger is a very complicated subject that needs to be unravelled. Four 'myths', in particular, about world hunger need to be challenged:

- **Myth 1 There is not enough food to go around.**   This is not true. The truth is that there is more than enough food in the world to feed everyone. It is quite possible for everyone to eat food containing 3000 calories a day, instead of the 1700 calories per day that millions try to survive on. The problem is that most of the food is in the wrong place and in the hands of the wrong people. Whilst 750 million people go hungry, Europe destroys 1,500 million tonnes of food each year. North America has only 6 per cent of the world's population (210 million people) yet it consumes, and wastes, 35 per cent of the world's resources.

Another problem is that even when a developing country produces food, its own population cannot afford to buy it. India, for example, with 50 per cent of the world's poorest people, still has a regular grain surplus of 25 tonnes. When their own people cannot buy the food, large landowners turn to growing 'cash crops', such as tobacco, tea or coffee, to sell on the world's markets.

- **Myth 2 World hunger is caused by over-population.**   It is true that the world's population is expanding and that this will cause many problems in the future. It is also true that the population is increasing fastest in the world's poorest countries. Yet, when the problem is looked at in terms of population density (the number of people living in a square kilometre) the situation looks different. In Western Europe the population density is 98 whilst in Africa it is just 19. The problem is that much of the land in poor countries is infertile and people cannot afford the technology needed to improve its fertility. As a result, overcrowded Western Europe is able to feed its population, whilst in sparsely populated Africa millions go hungry.

- **Myth 3 Starvation is the result of natural disasters.**   Natural disasters do not only affect developing countries but, when they do, these countries do not have the resources to deal with them. Disasters such as earthquakes, floods and droughts also hit developed countries but they have food, shelter and other resources in abundance.

- **Myth 4 Science will soon be able to cure world hunger.**   In the 1960s scientists worked hard to develop new strains of wheat and rice that would produce bigger harvests. During the so-called 'Green Revolution' these new strains were introduced into many developing countries. They brought some benefits with them but not the miraculous results that many people were hoping for.

Why is it a myth simply to say that world hunger is caused by over-population?

The conclusion is inescapable. The human race does have the means to tackle the almost overwhelming problem of world hunger and malnutrition. To do so, however, would involve the rich countries, including Britain and the USA, consuming, and wasting, far less than they do at the present time. The developed world spends just £20 billion a year on aid and over £500 billion on military weapons. Until this situation changes, millions of people will die unnecessarily each year.

WORK TO DO

1 Can you explain why each year millions of people throughout the world die of malnutrition, although there is more than enough food in the world to feed everyone?

2 Explain why world hunger is not simply the result of there being too many mouths in the world to feed.

3 Explain three causes of the widespread existence of hunger in today's world.

4 Christian Aid claims that this country's top ten supermarkets make more money in a year than the world's poorest 35 countries combined. What do you think the Christian response to this should be?

Extract 2

There is surely a moral imperative to bring sanity to this crazy deadly situation [about food wastage], to restore human dignity, to promote development and the possibility of peace. We must look at ourselves and our lifestyles. We must examine and change the processes and structures of the world which at the moment promote division and ultimately bring death.

Cardinal Basil Hume

DISCUSSION POINT

It seems that the answer to world hunger is simple – those who have too much must give to those who have too little. Could it possibly be that simple?

3.3 CAFOD

KEY QUESTION

What is CAFOD and what work does it do?

In 1962 the Catholic bishops in England and Wales set up CAFOD (Catholic Fund for Overseas Development). From its inception CAFOD has always tried to help the poor and disadvantaged throughout the world by helping them to help themselves. Projects financed by CAFOD attempt to tackle the causes, as well as the symptoms, of disease, ignorance and poverty. The goal of the organisation is to: 'Promote human development and social justice in witness to the Christian faith and gospel values.'

To this end, CAFOD now supports well over 500 different projects in more than 75 countries. The Irish equivalent of CAFOD is TROCAIRE ('mercy') and the two organisations often work alongside each other in their projects.

Extract 1

The duty of making oneself a neighbour to others and actively serving them becomes even more urgent when it involves the disadvantaged, in whatever area this might be. 'As you did it to one of the least of these my brethren, you did it to me.'

CCC (1932)

Tackling world development

CAFOD sets out to tackle many of the world's most pressing development issues by working along three interconnected lines.

1 Fundraising   To bring home the link between the money raised and the needs that it helps to meet, special sponsored fasts are held by CAFOD during Lent and October each year. On these special days church congregations and individuals are encouraged to go without food for a day and to give the money raised to CAFOD projects throughout the world. Each year more than £20 million is raised in this way to help the poor and disadvantaged.

2 Providing aid   As we saw earlier in 3.2, aid comes in two different, but equally important, forms:
- short-term aid. CAFOD can respond quickly when a natural disaster strikes or when a political situation, such as the recent wars in Bosnia and Kosovo, creates many refugees. The organisation is able to gather food, medicines and shelter so that it can respond within days. Often a number of charities in Britain, such as CAFOD, Christian Aid and Oxfam, launch a joint appeal for money when the need is particularly acute.
- long-term aid. Caritas is an international Catholic organisation that works on the ground in many countries. Much of the money raised by CAFOD is channelled through Caritas into various long-term projects which aim to improve health care, irrigation, food production, and education for both children and adults. Health workers take care and education to farmers and others who have no fixed home. In countries such as Brazil there are thousands, perhaps millions, of children living on the streets of most large cities. CAFOD supports workers who take education and other kinds of help to these street children.

Extract 2

I hope that, despite all obstacles, the generosity of your hearts will never weaken. I hope that through programmes such as the Catholic Fund for Overseas Development, you will continue to help the poor, to feed the hungry and to contribute to the cause of development. Always keep alive your Gospel tradition.

Pope John Paul II, speaking in Liverpool, 1982

3 Education   Educating people in Britain about development issues is a very important part of the work of CAFOD. The organisation spends 5p in every pound raised on educating Catholics in Britain, mainly through churches and schools, about the needs of developing countries. CAFOD workers go into schools to speak about various overseas projects and the organisation also produces resources for teachers to use.

Why get involved?

The struggle for equality and justice in the many poor parts of the world is one that should engage the hearts and minds of all Catholics. Following the example of Jesus they believe that the love of God needs to be taken everywhere. There is enough teaching in the Gospels and Epistles of the New Testament about justice and treating people with care and compassion to underline the conviction that this is an essential part of the Christian Gospel. Christians are called to work with God in creating a world that is less selfish and self-centred. If the Christian Gospel is what it claims to be then it is more than a personal way to salvation – it is the means by which God's purpose will be achieved in the whole world.

WORK TO DO

1 What was CAFOD set up to achieve and how does it set about reaching its objectives?

2 Explain how the work of CAFOD/TROCAIRE helps those people in today's world who are in greatest need.

3 Describe three ways in which CAFOD tries to help people in developing countries.

4 Roman Catholics support the work of CAFOD and TROCAIRE. What is there in the life and teaching of Jesus which might encourage them to do so?

DISCUSSION POINT

Someone might argue that the amount of help that charities like CAFOD can give is tiny compared to the great need in today's world – so it is hardly worth making the effort. Would you agree with them? What arguments could you put forward against them?

KEY WORDS

Bishop
Epistle
Gospel
Lent
New Testament

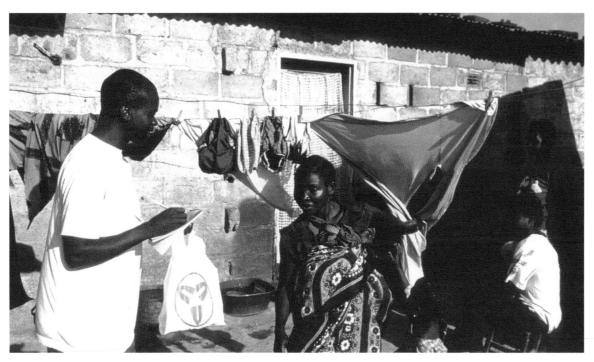

Do you think that the work of charities like CAFOD is important in the modern world?

3.4 THE SHEEP AND THE GOATS

KEY QUESTION

What can be learnt from the parable of the sheep and the goats about helping people who are in need?

CONSULT

Matthew 25:31–46

Extract 1

It is by what they have done for the poor that Jesus Christ will recognise his chosen ones.

CCC (2443)

Extract 2

The Church's love for the poor is part of her constant tradition. This love is inspired by the Gospel of the Beatitudes, of the poverty of Jesus and of his concern for the poor. Love for the poor is even one of the motives for the duty of working so as to be able to give 'to those in need'. It extends not only to material poverty but also to the many forms of cultural and religious poverty.

CCC (2444)

Matthew's Gospel contains a description of the gathering together of all people for judgement at the end of time. It is partly a parable – with the sheep, the goats and the shepherd – and partly a description of what will happen when the Son of Man (Jesus) returns to judge all nations. The description owes much to the Old Testament prophets, most notably Daniel (7:9–14) and Joel (3:2).

The sheep and the goats

Jesus said that when the Son of Man returns to judge he will separate the whole of mankind into two distinct groups.

1 The sheep – those whom he places on his right-hand side
The sheep, those who are 'blessed by my Father', will enter into the inheritance that God has planned for them 'since the creation of the world' (25:34). Jesus then went on to explain how those on his right hand will be chosen. They will be the people who, in this life, fed Jesus himself when he was hungry; gave him water to drink when he was thirsty; invited him into their house when he was a stranger and without friends; clothed him when he was naked; looked after him when he was sick and visited him when he was in prison.

The righteous question the Son of Man about this. When, they wonder, did they feed Jesus, give him a drink, invite him into their house, clothe him, look after him or visit him in prison? The answer of Jesus is instructive: 'I tell you the truth, whatever you did for one of the least of these brothers of mine, you did for me.' (25:40).

There has been much debate about the meaning of the phrase 'one of the least of these brothers of mine'. Some have thought that Jesus was simply referring to the disciples who received many acts of kindness when they were sent out to preach the Gospel. This, though, is unnecessarily restrictive. Jesus is clearly talking here about an important principle of all Christian service – that in meeting the needs of the poor, the hungry, the thirsty, the sick and the prisoner, a person is serving, and caring for, Christ himself.

2 The goats – those on the left hand of the Son of Man   These people are those who are consigned at the judgement to hell, 'into the eternal fire prepared for the devil and his angels' (25:41). What, though, is the crime that demands such a severe penalty? Unlike the sheep, the goats did not feed Jesus when he was hungry; give him water when he was thirsty; invite him in when he was a stranger; clothe him when he was naked or look after him when he was sick and in prison.

The goats, too, wondered when it was that they saw Jesus in such a condition and did not try to help him. The answer given by the Son of Man is uncompromising: 'I tell you the truth, whatever you did not do for one of the least of these, you did not do for me.' (25:45).

Works of charity and kindness given to people in need reflect just where people stand in relation to the kingdom of God, and to Jesus himself. Jesus identifies himself with the state and condition of all people, even the very least, and so makes compassion and concern for them equivalent to compassion directed towards himself. By saying this Jesus is emphasising a theme that runs throughout the Gospels – there is a close and integral link between religious worship and compassion to the poor shown in social action.

WORK TO DO

1 Jesus taught that the rich should share with the poor. That is the clear message in the story of the sheep and the goats.
  a) How do you think this story might encourage rich Christians to share what they have with the poor?
  b) Many Christians are reluctant to share what they have with the poor. Can you suggest some reasons for this and how you think they might react to the story of the sheep and the goats?

2 Explain what the parable of the sheep and the goats teaches about helping people who are in need.

3 Explain the link in the parable of the sheep and goats between helping a needy Jesus and helping those in need.

Extract 3

When we attend to the needs of those in want, we give them what is theirs, not ours. More than performing works of mercy, we are paying a debt of justice.

St Gregory the Great

DISCUSSION POINT

The story of the sheep and the goats underlines the very heavy penalties laid on those who do not look after the poor and the needy. Do you think that Jesus was being unnecessarily harsh in what he was saying?

KEY WORDS
Beatitudes
Disciples
Hell
Old Testament
Parable
Son of Man

Jesus often used parables to teach important truths. What do you think he wanted his listeners to learn from the parable of the sheep and goats?

4 CRIME AND PUNISHMENT

4.1 WHY PEOPLE BREAK THE LAW

KEY QUESTION

What is the law and why do people break it?

Extract 1

The Lord prescribed love towards God and taught justice towards neighbour, so that man would be neither unjust, nor unworthy of God. Thus, through the Decalogue [Ten Commandments] God prepared man to become his friend and to live in harmony with his neighbour . . . The words of the Decalogue remain likewise for us Christians. Far from being abolished, they have received amplification and development from the fact of the coming of the Lord [Jesus] in the flesh.

St Irenaeus

There has been a 'crime explosion' in the UK in recent years. In 1951 638,000 offences were reported to the police; in 1971 this figure had risen to 1.9 million; by 1986 it had reached 4.4 million and by 1998 the figure was well over 7 million. It is thought that for every crime reported three go unrecorded. If true, this would mean that around 30 million criminal offences are committed in the UK each year. Most of these crimes are carried out by people under the age of 25, with the highest rate being among people aged 16–19.

Breaking the law

Although many laws in this country go back a long time new laws are being made all the time by Parliament. As an example, barely 70 years ago people did not need to pass a test to drive a car. Now a large proportion of the total number of offences (some 25 per cent) are committed by motorists. New laws covering motoring are regularly being added to the statute book: for instance, it became illegal in 1996 to drive a coach faster than 56 mph on a motorway. The number of possible offences has increased considerably in recent years and this may explain some of the massive increase in the crime statistics.

The laws in this country can be divided into two categories:
- **indictable offences**   These are the most serious kinds of crime, including, for example, murder, manslaughter and rape.
- **non-indictable offences**   These are less serious crimes including petty theft and motoring offences.

Why, though, do so many people break the law? Several suggested answers have been put forward.

1 It is human nature.   Christians believe that all people are sinful from birth (a belief called 'original sin') and they express this human trait by breaking the law.

2 Satan leads people into temptation.   The increasing amount of crime reflects the breakdown of religious and moral standards in society, due to the activity of Satan.

3 Home background and the stresses of modern life are to blame.   We know that, in many instances, criminal activities such as drug-taking and vandalism are highest in areas where unemployment is also high.

4 Greed.   Advertisements stimulate the desire to have what we cannot afford. It is estimated that the average person working in a large city will see around 1000 advertisements for consumer goods during a single week. We cannot help being affected by what we see. For many people crime is the only way to obtain goods that they cannot acquire by legal means.

Law and order in the Bible

At a very early stage in Jewish history God gave the Jews many laws which covered all aspects of ethical and ritual (religious) behaviour. These laws were summed up in the Ten Commandments (see 1.2 and 1.3) which God wrote for Moses on two tablets of stone. The Jewish community was given the responsibility by God of punishing those who broke these laws – and some of the punishments were very harsh indeed. (You will find out more about this in 4.2.)

By the time of Jesus Jewish law was based on one simple principle – that human beings owe their highest allegiance to God and so they must deal fairly, but justly, with their fellow human beings. Jesus, though, introduced a new element in his teaching. He taught that compassion, and forgiveness, should be extended to those who had broken the law and had shown genuine repentance, as in the case of the woman caught in the act of adultery (see John 8:4). He also stressed the importance of inner motivation – a person might appear to keep the law but he or she could have committed adultery or murder in their hearts (Matthew 5: 38–48). This was a whole new way of thinking and one that his disciples took a considerable amount of time to understand.

WORK TO DO

1 a) How would you account for the fact that the number of crimes has increased so dramatically in recent years?
   b) Why do you think that many more people now seem prepared to break the law?

2 a) What new teaching about keeping the law did Jesus introduce?
   b) Why do you think that people found this teaching of Jesus very difficult to understand – and accept?

3 Prison is one of the ways in which we punish those who break the law. The New Testament writers often expressed an interest in the welfare of those in prison. What kind of sympathy do you think Christians should feel for those confined in this way?

Dramatic crimes make the headlines but an overwhelming proportion of crime is comparatively low key. Nearly all crime, though, hurts someone. Who really suffers when a crime is committed?

DISCUSSION POINT

Do you think that we deal in the best possible way with those who break the law in this country? Can you suggest any improvements that you would like to see in the ways that we punish criminals?

KEY WORDS

Adultery
Moses
Original sin
Satan
Ten Commandments

Who do you hold responsible for the great increase in the crime statistics?

Anyone found guilty of breaking the law in the UK is punished by a court of law. For minor offences, a fine or probation is the most likely outcome. For more serious offences a person may be sent to prison for a period which may be as little as a few days, or as long as life. Usually, in the case of a life sentence a judge recommends a minimum number of years that must be spent in jail. Only in a few extreme cases are criminals told that they will never be released from prison.

The purposes of punishment

1 Retribution   This simply means that all criminals deserve to be punished for their actions and punishment is the way that society takes its revenge on them. Some countries impose much harsher penalties than others. In Muslim countries, for instance, the death penalty is carried out for many offences other than murder, including rape, adultery and drug-trafficking. Although most countries have now abolished the death penalty (see 4.3) most parts of the USA still retain it for murder in certain circumstances.

2 Protection   Most people believe that society needs to be protected from people who threaten its stability. Locking a criminal away securely means that he or she can no longer threaten property or life.

3 Deterrence   Punishment is intended to stop criminals from committing further crimes and to deter others from following their example.

4 Reformation   Punishment should try to change the criminal so that he or she does not commit another crime. This is particularly true for young offenders. About 200,000 people aged 16–19 pass through the courts every year. A high proportion from this group continue on a life of crime. Prisons, though, are very overcrowded – there are now over 50,000 people in prison at any given time, occupying facilities originally built for fewer than 30,000. This makes the task of re-educating prisoners very difficult and over 75 per cent of all criminals re-offend after their release.

Extract 1

If anyone takes the life of a human being, he must be put to death. If anyone injures his neighbour, whatever he has done must be done to him: fracture for fracture, eye for eye, tooth for tooth. As he has injured the other so he is to be injured . . .

Leviticus 24:19–20

Judgement and forgiveness

The Christian approach is to stress the importance of both punishment and forgiveness. In the Old Testament the punishment aspect tended to be emphasised, as you can see from Extract 1. In the teaching of Jesus, however, the emphasis was very much upon non-violence and forgiveness. Whilst not directly repudiating the teaching of the Jewish Law (the Torah), Jesus suggested that there was a better way for people to take. This was the way of non-violence (see Extract 2). Jesus encouraged his followers not to judge others in case the same standards of judgement were applied against them. As he put it: 'Do not judge, or you will be judged. For in the same way as you judge others, you will be judged, and with the same measure you use, it will be measured to you.' (Matthew 7:1).

Extract 2

You have heard that it was said, 'Eye for eye and tooth for tooth'. But I tell you, Do not resist an evil person. If someone strikes you on the right cheek, turn to him the other also.

Matthew 5:38,39

Jesus based his whole life on the importance of forgiving others. When Peter asked Jesus how many times he should forgive someone who sinned against him he thought that he was being generous in suggesting that seven times was enough. Jesus, though, dismissed this 'generosity' by saying that he should forgive seventy times seven (Matthew 18:21). Jesus showed this forgiveness perfectly when, on the cross suffering the ultimate punishment for a crime he did not commit, he asked that those responsible for his death might be forgiven: 'Father, forgive them, for they do not know what they are doing.' (Luke 23:34).

In the Lord's Prayer Jesus taught his followers to pray 'Forgive us our debts, as we also have forgiven our debtors.' (Matthew 6:12). Such forgiveness is essential since, without it, bitterness gnaws away at a person. Forgiveness towards the criminal is difficult for people, especially the victim, to practise, but in the end it has to happen. Jesus taught that we can forgive others because God has first forgiven us. Being ready to forgive others is necessary for those who want to enter God's kingdom.

If putting a person in prison merely involves locking him or her up, is it a waste of time in the long run?

Work to do

1 Describe two aims that a society has when it punishes a criminal.

2 a) Choose one incident in the life of Jesus which shows his attitude towards those who have done wrong.
  b) What do you think Christians today can learn from the conversation between Jesus and Peter about forgiveness and the attitude they should adopt towards those who have broken the law?
  c) 'Christians should be more concerned for the victims of crime than for the criminals.' Do you think they should and have they sometimes got this wrong?

3 a) What is meant by retribution?
  b) Do you think that it is right, and necessary, to exact retribution upon those people who break the law?
  c) What form might that retribution take?

Discussion point

Christians try to maintain a balance between punishment and forgiveness. Do you think it is possible to do this when dealing with those people who have broken the law?

Key Words

Adultery
Lord's Prayer
Old Testament
Peter
Torah

4.3 THE DEATH PENALTY

KEY QUESTION

What is the attitude of the Catholic Church towards the death penalty?

The practice of putting people to death for committing certain very serious crimes is not a new one. The Romans crucified many criminals who were not Roman citizens and beheaded those who were. In eighteenth-century Britain there were over 200 offences, including some trivial ones, which carried the death sentence. In the years that followed, the death penalty was abolished for many of these offences but it remained for the crimes of:

- killing a policeman
- killing during an armed robbery
- killing by causing an explosion
- killing more than one person.

In 1965 Parliament suspended the death penalty for a trial period of five years and, in 1970, it was abolished except for a small number of crimes including treason.

As Extract 2 shows, the Catholic Church accepts that the death penalty might still be necessary in 'cases of extreme gravity'. There is considerable debate on this issue, though. In the USA, for example, where the death penalty is still used freely, the American bishops have declared that it is incompatible with any form of ethics which has 'respect for human life' at its centre. It is to the credit of many Christian nations that they have tried to follow the teaching of Jesus on forgiveness and have refrained from using the death penalty. By the end of 1998 67 countries had abolished the death penalty altogether and a further 14 have retained it only for exceptional crimes, like war offences. In 24 countries which still have the death penalty no executions have been carried out for the last ten years or more.

Extract 1

> Capital punishment is the ultimate cruel, inhuman and degrading punishment which violates the right to life . . .

Amnesty International

Arguments for capital punishment

Since 1970 several attempts have been made to reintroduce the death penalty in the UK but they have all been unsuccessful. These are the main arguments which have been put forward for its use:

- the death penalty is a tried and tested way of dealing with serious criminals, based on the Old Testament principle of 'An eye for an eye, a tooth for a tooth'.
- some people in our society only understand the language of violence. For these people the threat of the death penalty is the only deterrent likely to affect the way that they behave.
- society has a duty to protect those in the front line of the fight against crime, such as police officers, prison officers and so on. It must also protect those who are vulnerable and unable to protect themselves, such as children and old people.
- a 'life sentence' may turn out to be little longer than ten years. When a prisoner is released there is no guarantee that they will not murder again – although in practice this rarely happens.
- the death penalty means that justice can be seen to be done. The family and friends of a murdered person have the right to demand retribution.

People waiting outside a prison gate in the 1950s for news that a criminal had been executed. What do you think drew them there?

Arguments against the death penalty

- Only God has the right to give and take life.
- How can we be totally certain that someone is guilty? We now know of several people who have been executed in the past for crimes that they probably, or certainly, did not commit.
- There is no evidence to support the view that the death penalty is a real deterrent. In New York, for instance, where the death penalty is in operation the murder rate is 14 times higher than in London. The same pattern holds throughout the USA, where 68 criminals were executed in 1998.
- Executing terrorists would only turn them into martyrs.
- The death penalty is barbaric. Most countries have abandoned it. Although the death penalty remains in over 100 countries it is almost universally condemned.

WORK TO DO

1. a) What is capital punishment?
   b) It has been said that capital punishment should have no place in a civilised society. Do you agree?
   c) What arguments can you put forward in favour of maintaining the death penalty?
   d) What arguments can be put forward for abolishing the death penalty?

2. 'Christians can never agree with the death penalty. It would not have been the way of Jesus.' Do you agree with this comment? Give your reasons clearly.

PREJUDICE AND DISCRIMINATION

5.1 RACIAL PREJUDICE AND DISCRIMINATION

KEY QUESTION

What are racial prejudice and racial discrimination and how can they show themselves in our society?

Extract 1

Every form of social or cultural discrimination in fundamental personal rights on the grounds of sex, race, colour, social conditions, language or religion, must be curbed and eradicated as incompatible with God's design.

Second Vatican Council

Extract 2

Every human being created in the image of God is a person for whom Christ died. Racism, which is the use of a person's racial origin to determine a person's value, is an assault on Christ's values and a rejection of his sacrifice.

World Council of Churches, 1980

When we talk about racial prejudice and racial discrimination in the modern world there are four words which spring to mind. Each of these is central, in its own way, to the debate. A careful definition and understanding of them is essential if the discussion about them is to be conducted sensibly.

1 Racism   Racism is a belief in the superiority of one race over another. This superiority may be thought to be intellectual, physical or religious. If such a belief is strongly held then it can have an enormous influence over the way that one group sees, and treats, another.

2 Prejudice   Prejudice is a state of mind which encourages us to 'prejudge' others from a different racial group. If prejudice develops then the colour of a person's skin or their country of origin becomes the determining factor in our relationships with them. What we believe has a great influence on how we act. It is only a short step from believing one racial group to be inferior to treating them as such. Some of us inherit our prejudices from our parents or friends without thinking about them for ourselves. Often a prejudice is based on a single, unhappy experience that we, or someone else, has had of a particular racial group.

3 Stereotype   Prejudice and stereotyping are closely related. Stereotyping takes place when all members of one racial group are thought to share the same characteristics. These stereotypes are then used as the basis for racial abuse or discrimination.

4 Discrimination   If prejudice takes place in the mind then discrimination takes place in the real world. Discrimination happens when people are treated unfairly because of the colour of their skin or their country of origin. Many countries, including Britain (see 5.2), have passed laws to make discrimination in important areas such as housing, employment and education illegal. However, it is notoriously difficult to prove that someone did not get a job or lost a flat because of the colour of their skin.

Racism

Until comparatively recently geographical barriers such as oceans, mountains and rivers kept the different peoples apart. Each group developed its own national and racial characteristics – size and build, physical features and colour. Isolation allowed an attitude to develop which is still with us today and is at the heart of most racism – that of 'racial purity'. Like almost every other animal, human beings feel safest when they are surrounded by what they perceive to be their 'own kind'. 'Outsiders' are usually greeted with a mixture of suspicion and fear. Such fear, fuelled by an ignorance of those who are outwardly different, leads to racial hatred. It often lies dormant in individuals, and in society until something happens to stir it up. Racism can take two forms:

- it can be directed by individuals against other people. Racial attacks on ethnic minorities, for instance, are still commonplace in those areas where there is a large minority population. The most infamous example of this in Britain in the 1990s was the murder of Stephen Lawrence, a black teenager living in south-east London.
- it can be institutionalised. There were many examples of this during the twentieth century. In Germany during the 1930s the Nazis directed violent abuse against the Jewish population, which led in the early 1940s to the Holocaust in which over 6 million Jews were slaughtered. This kind of prejudice is called anti-Semitism. Then, between 1948 and 1994, a system of racial discrimination called apartheid was kept in place in South Africa, which allowed a white minority to deny almost every human right to the black majority population.

WORK TO DO

1 Explain the meaning of each of these words:
   a) prejudice
   b) racism
   c) stereotype
   d) discrimination.

2 Explain, in a sentence, the difference in meaning between prejudice and discrimination.

3 What is racial prejudice and why does it often lead to discrimination?

4 a) What is racism?
   b) How does racism often express itself in our society?

On what grounds do you think some people might object to a 'mixed marriage'? Do you agree with them?

Extract 3

God is black, a beautiful shining black. It is a wicked white man's lie to say that he is white. The Devil is white.

A Nigerian student

DISCUSSION POINT

Do you think that many people are prejudiced in our society? If so, where do you think such prejudice comes from?

KEY WORDS

Anti-Semitism
Apartheid
Holocaust

5.2 RACE RELATIONS IN BRITAIN

KEY QUESTION

How has Britain become a multi-ethnic and multi-religious society?

CONSULT

Leviticus 19:33,34

Extract 1

When an alien lives with you in your land, do not ill-treat him. The alien living with you must be treated as one of your native-born. Love him as yourself, for you were aliens in Egypt. I am the Lord your God.

Leviticus 19:33–34

People have been coming from other countries to settle in Britain for centuries. Roman, Viking and Norman invaders all intermingled and intermarried with the early inhabitants of this country. They have left their imprint on Britain's landscape, language, way of life and culture. Over the centuries there have been two main reasons why so many immigrants have settled in Britain:

1 To find work During the early nineteenth century many Irish immigrants moved into this country to find work building houses, roads and railways. The majority of them settled here permanently in towns such as Liverpool and Glasgow. Without them Britain would not have the transport infrastructure which it has today. In the 1950s and 1960s the British Government encouraged people from the Caribbean, India and Pakistan to emigrate to this country to live and work. They were brought here because the Second World War had robbed the country of millions of men and women. Thousands came and ended up doing those jobs that no one else was prepared to tackle.

2 To escape persecution It was for this reason that many Jews and Poles fled to Britain before, during and after the Second World War. In the 1970s many Asians fled from Uganda to find a safe refuge in Britain. Boat people from Vietnam and Kurds from Turkey also arrived in Britain during the 1970s and 1980s for the same reason. Britain has a strong tradition of offering a safe refuge to people who are in danger of persecution at home.

Many immigrants found it difficult to find accommodation so they settled in the poorer parts of cities like London, Manchester and Birmingham. As friends and relatives followed them 'ethnic communities' began to spring up. Today there are about 2.5 million black people in Britain, some 4 per cent of the total population. Tougher legislation was introduced in the 1970s and the 1980s to limit the number of immigrants allowed into the country. The flood of the 1960s is now barely a trickle.

The law and race relations

Ever since immigration started in earnest soon after the end of the Second World War, immigrants, particularly black immigrants, have faced abuse, harassment and violence. In 1976 the Race Relations Act attempted to protect every black citizen in Britain from racial discrimination by giving them the right to equal opportunities in employment, housing and education. It became illegal to discriminate in any area of life against a black person. It also made 'incitement to racial hatred' a criminal offence for the first time in Britain.

The Race Relations Act was a major step forward in improving the lives of black people in Britain. Yet it seems to have had little impact on changing people's minds and hearts. A Social Attitudes Survey (1998) conducted in Britain found that:
- 35 per cent of people interviewed described themselves as racially prejudiced.
- 66 per cent of people in the survey were convinced that they had been denied a job or a place to live at some time because of the colour of their skin.

Christians and race

In 5.3 we will look at the example of Jesus and the teaching of the New Testament about racial prejudice and discrimination. In 5.4 we turn our attention to one of the most well-known parables of Jesus – the Good Samaritan – which has a powerful point to make about discrimination. Here we make the simple observation that when large numbers of immigrants came to live in Britain in the 1950s and 1960s they were not given a particularly warm welcome by the largely all-white churches. Instead, black people set up their own churches which have flourished whilst other churches have languished in the 1980s and 1990s.

WORK TO DO

1 'All people living in this country should enjoy the same rights, whatever their race or religion.'
   a) Do you agree?
   b) Why?

2 a) Give two examples of racial discrimination that might be found in Britain today.
   b) Why do you think it is extremely difficult to eradicate racial discrimination altogether by passing laws against it?

3 a) What do you think a Christian's attitude should be towards people of other races who live in Britain?
   b) What positive steps do you think the Christian Church could take to improve race relations in Britain?

Extract 2

The Church reproves, as foreign to the mind of Christ, any discrimination against people . . . on the basis of their race, colour, condition in life or religion.

Second Vatican Council

DISCUSSION POINT

In what practical ways might churches and individual Christians work towards eliminating racial discrimination and prejudice in their own areas?

KEY WORDS
Immigrant
Parables

Do you agree with the observation that if black and white are ever to live together in true harmony then we have to begin with children and young people?

5.3 JESUS AND DISCRIMINATION

KEY QUESTION

What did Jesus have to say about racial prejudice and discrimination in its different forms?

CONSULT

Luke 7:1–10;
Mark 5:1–20;
Acts 11:1–18

Jesus was brought up in a multiracial and multicultural society. The Jews were a minority group in their own country, probably making up no more than 30 per cent of the overall population of Palestine. Since 163 BCE the Jews had lived under Roman rule and alongside many Greek communities. From his earliest years Jesus would have had day-to-day contact with many non-Jews (Gentiles) and this continued throughout his ministry. He rejected the narrow exclusivity preached by religious groups such as the Pharisees and the Sadducees, and told the people that the kingdom of God was open to all. Jesus taught that this kingdom would attract people from the north and south, east and west (see Extract 1).

The Roman army officer

Mark tells us how a Roman army officer in Capernaum had a much-loved servant who was desperately ill. He heard of Jesus and sent some elders from the Jewish synagogue to him to see whether he would heal his servant. The Roman officer assumed that Jesus would not even talk to him as he was a Gentile. The elders told Jesus that the Roman officer 'deserves to have you do this, because he loves our nation and has built our synagogue' (Luke 7:5). The man is presented by Mark as a person of the highest integrity, as demonstrated by his concern for his slave, his attitude to the Jews and his feeling of unworthiness in the presence of Jesus.

Yet it is the man's faith that stands out most clearly. The friends of the man reported his farewell words to Jesus: 'Lord, don't trouble yourself, for I do not deserve to have you come under my roof . . . say the word and my servant will be healed.' (Luke 7:6,7). Jesus was very impressed by what he heard. He told the crowd: 'I have not found such great faith even in Israel [i.e. amongst his fellow Jews].' By his actions in healing this man's servant, a Gentile, Jesus underlined the truth found in the later words of St Paul (see Extract 2). In God's kingdom no distinction at all is drawn between Jews and Gentiles – all are equal.

Religious prejudice

As well as using the parable of the Good Samaritan (see 5.4) with its clear teaching on religious prejudice, Jesus demonstrated that his message and concern crossed all national and religious barriers in another incident. In Mark 5:1–20 we read how Jesus helped a non-Jewish man in Gerasa who was possessed by many evil spirits. The man screamed at Jesus to leave him alone but Jesus sent the spirits out of the man and into some pigs nearby who stampeded into the sea and were drowned. A background note to this incident is that Jews were not allowed by the law given to them by Moses to keep pigs because the eating of pork was forbidden.

Extract 1

At that time men will see the Son of Man coming in the clouds with great power and glory. And he will send his angels and gather his elect [chosen ones] from the four winds, from the ends of the earth to the ends of the heavens.

Mark 13:26,27

The apostles, after the Day of Pentecost, were slow to grasp the truth that the message of Jesus, the Gospel, was for all people, whether Jews or Gentiles. Peter did not come to this truth easily. Then he had a vision (Acts 11:1–18) in which he saw a large sheet being let down from heaven containing all kinds of birds, animals and reptiles, including those that Jews were not allowed to eat. A voice told Peter to kill and eat any of the animals in the sheet. From this, Peter understood that the Gospel message that he preached was intended for people of all nations and not just the Jews.

The implications of these examples from the New Testament are clear. God created all human beings. Everyone, whatever their race or creed, is equal in God's sight. It is totally wrong to treat any human being as inferior to another and this is what happens when we are prejudiced. Jesus rejected the prejudices of his day and this is the example that all Christians should follow. He welcomed, without discrimination, all who came to him for help. The first Christians learned through experience to follow his example. Christians today must belong to a Church which is truly open to everyone, without any prejudice or discrimination.

WORK TO DO

1 What might Christians today learn from the Bible about how to oppose racial discrimination?

2 a) Briefly outline Peter's dream about clean and unclean food.
   b) What do you think this dream has to teach Christians today about treating all people equally?

3 Give an account of the biblical teaching which Catholics might use in forming their views about racism and explain how these teachings are important for Catholics living in today's world.

Extract 2

Here [in Christ] there is no Greek nor Jew, circumcised or uncircumcised, barbarian, Scythian, slave or free, but Christ is all, and is in all.

Colossians 3:11

DISCUSSION POINT

What do you think might have happened to the Christian faith if Jesus and the early Christians had not made it clear that it was intended for all people, whatever their religious and racial background?

KEY WORDS

Apostle
Day of Pentecost
Gentile
Moses
New Testament
Parable
Peter
Synagogue

Do you think that the Church today is truly welcoming to all people, whatever their racial background? Can you think of any improvements the Church could make?

5.4 THE GOOD SAMARITAN

KEY QUESTION

What did Jesus teach about prejudice and discrimination through the parable of the Good Samaritan?

CONSULT

Luke 10:25–37

Extract 1

Give to everyone who asks of you, and if anyone takes what belongs to you do not demand it back. Do to others as you would have them do to you.

Luke 6:30–31

Extract 2

One cannot honour another person without blessing God his Creator. One cannot adore God without loving all men, his creatures.

CCC

An expert in the Jewish law asked Jesus, 'What must I do to inherit eternal life?' The man addressed Jesus as 'teacher' (rabbi) and asked a question about eternal life – both indicating a degree of respect for Jesus' views. In good Jewish fashion Jesus pointed the questioner back to the Ten Commandments which were the ultimate source of religious knowledge for every Jew.

Jesus simply asked the man: 'What is written in the Law? How do you read it?' In reply the lawyer gives the same answer that Jesus himself had given in Mark 12:29–31. On that occasion Jesus had been asked which was the greatest of all the commandments and this summary was clearly accepted by Jews at the time as summing up the whole of their precious Law. The summary given by the man here is twofold:

- 'Love the Lord your God with all your heart and with all your soul and with all your mind.' (11:27)
- 'Love your neighbour as yourself.' (11:27)

Jesus approved: 'You have answered correctly . . . Do this and you will live.' Jesus had a very high respect for the Jewish law. Like all Jews, he believed that anyone who lived perfectly by the demands of the Ten Commandments would have eternal life.

The parable

The lawyer wished to take his conversation with Jesus a stage further. Who, he wondered, was really his 'neighbour'? To answer this question Jesus told him his most well-known parable – that of the Good Samaritan. The parable was set by Jesus on the steep road, 27 km long, which descended 1000 m from Jerusalem to Jericho, a town which was the country dwelling of priests who were not on duty in Jerusalem. The hatred between Jews and Samaritans went back for centuries and Jesus' listeners would not have missed the significance of the story.

The road was a favourite haunt of robbers and the story of a Jewish traveller being attacked, and left for dead, was a familiar one. The first two characters in the story, a priest and a Levite (a worker in the Temple in Jerusalem) may have feared defiling themselves by coming into contact with a dead body – as the Jewish law taught. No motive for their behaviour, however, is given. The third character is a Samaritan who 'took pity on him' (Luke 10:33). This response was not only a stark contrast to that of the priest and the Levite but also unexpected in the light of the centuries-old hostility between Jews and Samaritans. The pity felt by the Samaritan is soon translated into action – he probably used his own clothing to make bandages, his own wine as a disinfectant and his own oil as a soothing lotion. He put the man on his own donkey and paid the inn-keeper to look after him out of his own pocket.

Parables and decision-making

The parables in the Gospels were intended to lead the listeners to a point of decision. In response to the question asked by the lawyer, Jesus focused on the person who loved, the Samaritan who became a neighbour by what he did. The lawyer is forced to admit that true love is not limited in its scope but is unlimited in its application. Furthermore, love will always express itself in action, in this case an act of mercy, which might prove to be costly in different ways. For the 'expert in the law' this was a dramatic reversal of understanding. He would have thought of the Jewish victim as a 'good' person and the Samaritan as evil. To a Jew there was no such thing as a 'good' Samaritan. Jesus, though, underlined, the basic thrust of his teaching. 'Go and do likewise,' he told the man. There is no room for prejudice or discrimination of any kind in the kingdom of God. Those who refuse to love others, whatever their creed or social background, cannot hope to enter God's kingdom. To reject anyone in need, and to refuse to love, shows that a person has not recognised just how much they themselves need God's love.

WORK TO DO

1 a) Recount, in your own words, the story of the Good Samaritan told by Jesus.
   b) What do you think that we can learn from this parable about prejudice and discrimination in the modern world?

2 a) Who asked Jesus a question about eternal life?
   b) How did this person show his respect for Jesus?
   c) What answer did Jesus give him?
   d) Where did the parable of the Good Samaritan fit in?

Extract 3

Jesus shares the life of the poor, from the cradle to the cross; he experiences hunger, thirst and privation. Jesus identifies with the poor of every kind and makes active love towards them the condition of entering his kingdom.

CCC (544)

DISCUSSION POINT

How would you answer the question 'What must I do to inherit eternal life?' today?

KEY WORDS

Gospel
Parable
Rabbi
Temple
Ten Commandments

A stained-glass window showing scenes from the parable of the Good Samaritan. The CCC in Extract 3 talks about active love. What do you think this means and how was it displayed by the Good Samaritan?

5.5 AGEISM

KEY QUESTION

What is ageism and why is it unfair?

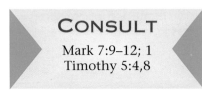

CONSULT

Mark 7:9–12; 1 Timothy 5:4,8

Extract 1

Do not rebuke an older man harshly . . . If a widow has children or grandchildren, these should learn first of all to put their religion into practice by caring for their own family and so repaying their parents and grandparents . . . If anyone does not provide for relatives, and especially for his immediate family, he has denied the faith and is worse than an unbeliever.

1 Timothy 5:1–8

Extract 2

It ought to be lovely to be old,
To be full of the peace that comes from experience
And wrinkled ripe fulfilment.

D.H. Lawrence, Selected Poems

In the UK more and more people are surviving well into old age. This is due mainly to great improvements in our general standard of living and health care, combined with the wider availability of facilities for the elderly. Look at these statistics about old age:

- 17 per cent of the population of the UK is now past retiring age – more than 10 million people in all. During the twentieth century the number of people living beyond the age of 65 increased by over 400 per cent. The life expectancy for men is now 70 and for women 75.
- the State pension is only 30 per cent of the average working wage, and decreasing all the time, so more and more old people will live in poverty. Some 2 million households are made up of old people living alone, with 500,000 old people having no living relative. Two of the major problems facing old people are those of loneliness and depression.

Ageism

Just as we have racial discrimination (5.1 and 5.2) and sexual discrimination (5.6), so we have ageism. This is discrimination against a person because of their age. Compulsory retirement of women at 60 and men at 65 is a form of ageism since it is based on the premise that when a person reaches a certain age they are no longer capable of working. Many old people look forward to retirement but others would like to be given the choice. For many the sudden transition from work to retirement is too swift. It would help them if retirement could be introduced gradually through part-time work.

Age discrimination, like other forms of discrimination, can lead to stereotyping. Stereotypes are 'fixed pictures' in the mind about all people in a certain group. Here are some typical stereotypes about old age.

- 'Old people are always living in the past.'
- 'Old people never have a good word to say about young people. They are always criticising.'
- 'Old people are always a burden on their children and grandchildren.'

You can see straightaway how unfair these stereotypes are. Stereotypes are always unfair because they are based on ignorance.

Then and now

Ageism is also seen in the way in which the elderly are often treated in our society. Within the old Jewish extended family system, reflected in the Bible, the patriarchal (grandfather/father) and matriarchal (grandmother/mother) figures stood at the head of their clan or family. Younger family members were taught to respect them and see them as the possessors of great wisdom, derived from many years of experience. They were consulted when important family decisions had to be taken and so they felt that they had a continuing, and important, role to play in family life. This role has long since disappeared. Most elderly people feel that their opinions are no longer valued. It is the younger members of the family who now take all the responsibility and make all the decisions. By dispensing with the services of the elderly, and taking decisions on their behalf, we are contributing to ageism. Apart from the elderly in our own family, few of us have any real contact with old people around us. Little wonder, then, that so many old people feel isolated and useless. All of this could be storing up immense problems for the future. One in every six people in Britain is now elderly. By the year 2025 this will be reflected worldwide. Some way has to be found to look after so many old people, so that they can make a real contribution to the society in which they live.

WORK TO DO

1 a) What is stereotyping?
   b) List five ways in which elderly people are often stereotyped in our society.

2 a) How has the age structure of our society changed during the twentieth century?
   b) What are the major problems associated with growing old?
   c) Why do you think that an ageing population might cause problems in the future?

3 a) What do you understand by 'ageism'?
   b) Why do you think that ageism is very unfair to the elderly?

How well do you think we treat elderly people in our society?

DISCUSSION POINT

How do you think that holding Christian moral values might affect the way that a family, or a society, treats its elderly members?

If people are going to live longer and longer, what kind of role in society do you think they should be given as they grow older?

5.6 SEXISM

KEY QUESTION

What is sexism?

Sexism, like racism and ageism, is all about prejudice and discrimination. This time, though, the issue is not one of age or colour but gender. Sexism is based on the premise that, in one way or another, one gender (usually male) is better than the other (usually female). The attitude is founded on some form of sexual stereotyping in which women are seen solely as mothers or the objects of male sexual desire (see Extract 1).

Extract 1

A woman should remain at home, sit still, keep house and bring up children.

Martin Luther, sixteenth-century religious reformer

Sexual stereotyping

Sexual stereotyping can be very subtle. The fact that most women are mothers has led many men to think that there are jobs for which women are more 'naturally' suited than men. These jobs are those which call upon the same kinds of skill that a woman needs to be a good mother. Nursing, teaching small children and child care are three examples.

It may not be harmful to think in this way. It might even be true to say that there are certain jobs which are more suited to men or to women. Some jobs, for example, may require a degree of physical strength that most women do not have. For many women, though, this way of thinking is dangerous because it shuts doors and denies them the opportunity to do what they want to do with their own lives. As long as society, or the Church, simply looks on women as potential wives or mothers then any woman who wants to find a different role in life will have many problems to overcome.

Extract 2

I want men everywhere to pray . . . also want women to dress modestly, with decency and propriety, not with braided hair or gold or pearls or expensive clothes, but with good deeds, appropriate for women who profess to worship God. A woman should learn in quietness and full submission. I do not permit a woman to teach or have authority over a man; she must be silent . . . But women will be saved through childbearing – if they continue in faith, love and holiness with propriety.

1 Timothy 2:8–15

The Sex Discrimination Act, 1975

Since 1975 it has been illegal to discriminate against women in the areas of:
- recruitment for work
- promotion at work
- training for work.

In the same year, the Employment Protection Act made it illegal to dismiss a woman simply because she had become pregnant. Under the Act every woman worker was entitled to maternity leave if she wanted to take it. Why, then, are there far fewer women than men in top jobs?

- Many women do find it difficult to combine a demanding job with bringing up a family. Some businesses are unwilling to appoint a woman if they think there is a possibility she might become pregnant in the near future, in case she decides to leave.
- Businesses take little notice of the needs of women with children – few companies offer crèche facilities for employees' children, for example. Only a handful of companies allow flexible working hours to fit in with the school hours of children.
- Maternity leave is expensive for a company if it needs to find a trained replacement. Many companies find it easier, and cheaper, to appoint a man in the first place.

Prejudice against women

The problem of prejudice against women goes back to the Bible. In the Old Testament men had a dominant role in society and this is carried over into the New Testament and the teaching of the early Christian Church. Paul insisted that all women should cover their heads and keep silent in Christian worship, and accept the domination of their husbands in the marriage relationship (see Extract 2). Later Church leaders carried this much further, finding little that was positive to say about women (see Extract 3).

In 1992 the Church of England voted to allow women to become priests thus following the example set by several other Churches. The Roman Catholic Church, however, stated its clear opposition to women's ordination in 1976 and this position has been underlined more than once by Pope John Paul II. This opposition is based on the long tradition of the Church, the impossibility of a woman representing Christ at the Mass, and the teaching of the Holy Scriptures. The fact that other Churches have decided to ordain women has been put forward as a major stumbling-block towards closer relationships in the future between these Churches and the Catholic Church.

WORK TO DO

1 a) Give one example of how sexual stereotyping can take place.
 b) Why is sexual stereotyping dangerous?

2 What did the Sex Discrimination and Employment Protection Acts of 1975 set out to do?

3 Why are there fewer women in top jobs than men?

4 Do you hold the Bible, and the Church, responsible for prejudice against women? Explain your answer.

Extract 3

Every woman should be overwhelmed with shame at the thought that she is a woman.

Clement of Alexandria, a bishop of the early Church

DISCUSSION POINT

Bearing in mind Extracts 1–3, it seems that the Church is responsible for much of the past prejudice against women. Do you agree?

KEY WORDS

Church of England
Mass
New Testament
Old Testament
Paul

Do you think that sexism will gradually die out, or is it likely to be a continuing problem?

5.7 THE DISABLED

KEY QUESTION

Who are the disabled in our country and what problems do they have?

Extract 1

They came to Bethsaida, and some people brought a blind man and begged Jesus to touch him. He took the blind man by the hand and led him outside the village. When he had spat on the man's eyes and put his hands on him Jesus asked, 'Do you see anything?' He looked up and said, 'I see people; they look like trees walking around.' Once more Jesus put his hands on the man's eyes. Then his eyes were opened, his sight was restored and he saw everything clearly. Jesus sent him home saying, 'Do not go into the village.'

Mark 8:22–26

The word 'disabled' itself refers to the loss of the full use of any limb or part of the body. Under this umbrella term the disabled can be divided into two broad categories:

- **people with learning difficulties.** There are 500,000 people in the UK who have learning difficulties (also known as mental handicap). MENCAP (The Royal Society for Mentally Handicapped Children and Adults) is the largest organisation in this country specially committed to meeting the needs of this large group of people.

- **people with physical disabilities.** In the UK one in twelve people (over 4 million people) suffers from some kind of physical disability. Sixty per cent of the world's disabled people, though, are found in developing countries. The majority receive no help apart from that given by relatives and friends. Most have no chance of employment and many end up begging in the streets.

The International Year of the Disabled

In 1971 the United Nations set out the rights of people with learning difficulties and, four years later, they did the same for those who are physically disabled. Then, in 1981, an International Year of the Disabled was declared to bring the needs of disabled people to the attention of as many people as possible. It was given the motto 'Full Participation and Equality' – underlining the basic human rights which all disabled people have a right to expect.

Five objectives were set for the year. Although much progress has been made, many of these objectives have still to be met in different places. The objectives are:

1 to help physically and mentally handicapped people to become fully adjusted to life.

2 to support all national and international efforts to train and educate disabled people to lead as full a life as possible. Disabled people, have the same rights to full employment as able-bodied people.

3 to encourage shops and public places to make access for disabled people as easy as possible.

4 to educate the general public about the rights and needs of disabled people.

5 to prevent disability as much as possible and to help with the physical and emotional rehabilitation of disabled people.

Cheshire Homes

Many charities have been set up to meet the needs of people with different forms of disability. Most of them concentrate on one kind of disability so that they are able to offer specialist help in that area. Amongst this large number of charities, few have been established as long, or been able to offer such practical help, as the Cheshire Homes. Group Captain Leonard Cheshire, a Roman Catholic, was a hero of the Second World War who witnessed the dropping of the atomic bombs on the Japanese cities of Hiroshima and Nagasaki. He found this experience intensely disturbing and he wanted to do something useful with his life when the war ended.

Cheshire believed that he had a 'vocation' from God to help those who were physically disabled or ill. By 1959 he had set up 23 homes in different countries. By 1992, the year of Cheshire's death, there were 270 such homes in 51 different countries. In the UK 37 Cheshire Family Support Services were also providing day-to-day care for people with disabilities who were able to live in their own homes.

DISCUSSION POINT

Do you think that the parents of children with disabilities should be encouraged to send them to a school for able-bodied children, or would they be better off in a school for children with similar problems?

KEY WORD
Vocation

WORK TO DO

1 a) Why do you think that the International Year of the Disabled set out to educate the able-bodied about the needs of disabled people, as well as seeking actually to meet those needs?

   b) Do you think that able-bodied people are well informed about and ready to help meet the needs of those who are disabled?

2 a) Why do you think that some people choose to work amongst the physically disabled and people with learning difficulties?

   b) Is it the kind of work that you would enjoy doing? Explain your answer.

3 What do you think the United Nations meant by its motto 'Full Participation and Equality' for disabled people?

What kind of help do you think this man needs to help him live a fully satisfying life?

5.8 THE PARABLE OF THE TALENTS

KEY QUESTION

What did Jesus say in the parable of the talents and what did he want his listeners to learn from it?

CONSULT

Matthew 25:14–30;
Luke 19:11–27

Extract 1

> Well done, good and faithful servant! You have been faithful with a few things; I will put you in charge of many things. Come and share your master's happiness.

Matthew 25:23

Extract 2

> I tell you that to everyone who has, more will be given, but as for the one who has nothing, even what he has will be taken away.

Luke 19:26

The central theme of the parable of the talents – a master going away and leaving his servants with responsibilities to fulfil in his absence – was used by Jesus more than once. In Matthew 24:45–51; the master also goes away for a long time and the theme of the parable is to ask who will be ready when the master returns. In the parable of the talents, however, the important issue is what the three servants have done in his absence.

The parable

A talent was simply a large sum of money – many thousands of pounds in modern coinage. It has acquired, though, a metaphorical meaning which applies it to those God-given talents and abilities that we are responsible for using. A different number of talents was given to each servant 'according to his ability'. The return that the master expected from his money was in proportion to the ability of each servant. God recognises that we are all different and only expects from us what is appropriate. Note two things about the parable:

1 one servant is given five talents and another is given two. Both double their master's gift whilst he is away. He gives to the two of them exactly the same commendation when he returns and sees what they have done: 'Well done, good and faithful servant.' Both these servants are given, as a reward, a share in their master's 'happiness'. Jesus is suggesting that eternity in his everlasting kingdom will bring new responsibilities and eternal delight.

2 the third servant buries the talent that he is given by his master because he is afraid to invest it and multiply it by sensible work. He is afraid that if he were to lose the talent then his master would be angry with him. His master is angry. He condemns him for not being willing to take a risk and use his talent. He takes the talent away from the man and gives it to the servant who has most. The lazy servant is thrown into the darkness of hell where there is, according to Jesus, weeping and gnashing of teeth.

Understanding the parable

The message of the parable and its relevance to the matters that have concerned us in this unit need to be teased out. God created us in our mother's womb and bestowed on us different gifts or talents. One of those gifts was our health and strength – a gift denied, for some reason known only to God, to a large number of people. From those people to whom many talents are given, much is expected. God intends that they should go out, carry responsibility and work towards the building of his kingdom on earth by investing in productive work all the talents that God has given to them. Those who do so are rewarded at the end of this life with eternal joy and life spent in the presence of God. Those who receive any talents from God and bury them in the ground, because they are afraid to use them, will spend eternity apart from God. That is the chilling message of this parable.

Even those who have severe physical disabilities or learning difficulties have been given talents by God to use. Many bring great joy and pleasure into the lives of their families and those who look after them. Quite simply, they are a God-given blessing. This is why Roman Catholics are totally opposed to any form of abortion which would offer future parents the opportunity of aborting a foetus known to be severely physically or mentally handicapped. The law in Britain allows a woman to seek an abortion for this reason but the Catholic Church is totally opposed to abortion on any grounds whatsoever. God is not a hard taskmaster – the third servant was wrong. He does, however, expect and reward the use of the creative opportunities that are open to us for service. If we have been blessed with our full health and strength then we carry a heavy responsibility to use our gifts responsibly and adventurously. That is the only way to be ready for the coming of the Son of Man at the end of the age.

Do you think that the master in the parable is being hard on the servant who buried his gift?

WORK TO DO

1 a) Tell the parable of the talents in your own words.
   b) What do you think Jesus was trying to teach through this parable?

2 a) Describe what, according to Jesus, happened to the three servants in the parable of the talents.
   b) Do you think that the treatment of the third servant by his master was fair or not? Explain your answer.

3 What do you think we can learn from the parable of the talents about the importance of the disabled in our society?

DISCUSSION POINT

Imagine that you discover in the future that you are to be the parent of a disabled baby. What do you think your reaction to the news would be? Do you agree with the teaching of the Catholic Church that an abortion is sinful, whatever the health of the unborn child might be?

KEY WORDS

Abortion
Parable
Son of Man

6 WAR AND PEACE

6.1 WAR AND PEACE

A war is any conflict in which the regular armed forces of at least one of the participants is involved – and which lasts longer than 60 minutes. That is the official definition.

KEY QUESTION

What are the main reasons why nations go to war against each other?

CONSULT

Isaiah 11:6;
Matthew 5:38,39
and 26:52

Wars in the twentieth century

Wars in the twentieth century can be distinguished from earlier conflicts simply because there has been many more of them. They have also had the capacity to inflict much more serious damage than earlier conflicts.

It is estimated that wars fought during the twentieth century alone claimed the lives of more than 100 million people – soldiers and civilians. There were 9 million fatalities in the First World War (1914–18) and 55 million people died in the Second World War (1939–45). Since 1945 there have been over 250 wars in different parts of the world. As soon as the flames die down in one place they flare up in another. In an average year there are at least five armed conflicts.

The number of people injured in war during the twentieth century is thought to be at least five times greater than the number of those killed – c.100 million. In the First World War 21 million injuries were reported. People were still dying as a direct result of their injuries 40 years later. Over 200 million injuries were sustained during the Second World War.

The nature of the casualty list has changed as bigger and better weapons have been developed. In the First World War 95 per cent of casualties were soldiers but by the Second World War this had dropped to below 50 per cent. In the ever-growing list of civil wars there are nine civilian casualties for every soldier killed. Furthermore, it is civilians who suffer most from the inevitable destruction of towns and farmland, water supplies, housing, hospitals and schools that war brings in its wake. There are now some 16 million refugees in the world, without a home or country, and almost all of these lost everything through war, civil or otherwise. In the 1999 conflict in Kosovo alone some 1.75 million people became refugees almost overnight. When they returned to their homes they found almost total devastation.

Extract 1

You will hear of wars and rumours of wars but see to it that you are not alarmed. Such things must happen but the end is still to come.

Matthew 24:6

Why do people fight?

- **Civil war**   Often a political group within a country uses violent means to oppose the government of that country. In recent years such countries as Sudan, Afghanistan, El Salvador and Rwanda have been totally disrupted by civil conflict. The human cost is immense, with millions left starving and homeless. Many of the most distressing recent famines have come about as a direct result of civil wars.

- **Disputes over borders and frontiers**   Sometimes two countries lay claim to the same territory. Usually this territory is land, although it can be a stretch of water. For example, ever since the creation of the separate states of India and Pakistan in 1947, the two countries have both claimed the region of Kashmir. In 1999 armed clashes were still taking place on the borders of the two countries. Often there are disputes over territories because the disputed area contains valuable resources such as oil and gas.

- **Wars between nations**   Since the end of the Second World War there have been many conflicts in the Middle East and South-East Asia, including the Korean War (1950–53); the Vietnam War (1965–73); the war between Iran and Iraq (1980–88) and the Gulf War (1991). Since 1945 only one year has passed, 1968, when the British Army has not been involved in armed conflict somewhere.

WORK TO DO

1 How did Jesus say that his followers should treat their enemies?

2 a) Jesus told his followers that they should 'turn the other cheek' when faced with aggression. What do you think he meant when he said this?
   b) Give one example of a situation in which it might be appropriate for a Christian to turn the other cheek.
   c) Do you think that this advice of Jesus is appropriate in the modern world?

3 a) 'Christians believe that peace is always better than war.' Do you agree with this?
   b) What reasons do you think lie behind this point of view?

Extract 2

Respect for and development of human life require peace. Peace is not merely the absence of war and it is not limited to maintaining a balance of powers between adversaries. Peace cannot be attained on earth without safeguarding the goods of persons, free communication between men, respect for the dignity of persons and peoples, and the assiduous practice of fraternity. Peace is 'the tranquillity of order'. Peace is the work of justice and the effect of charity.

CCC (2304)

DISCUSSION POINT

Do you have any realistic hope that war will become redundant in your lifetime? Give reasons for your opinion.

Isaiah (11:6–9) said that in God's kingdom natural enemies in the animal kingdom would lie down peacefully together. Why do you think that peace between nations is so difficult to achieve?

6.2 THE 'JUST WAR'

KEY QUESTION

What is the theory of the 'just war' and how does it work?

The fifth commandment plainly forbids murder (see 1.3). The Beatitudes tell us that it is the peacemakers who will be called God's children (see 1.5). These verses encourage the Roman Catholic Church to call on people everywhere to pray continually for peace and to do everything in their power to avoid war.

War, a last resort

As a last resort, however, the Catholic Church has always taught that governments have the right, and the authority, to declare war to defend their own citizens or, in certain situations, citizens living in another country. The apostle Paul argued that the governing authorities have been put in place by God and so have the authority to take the necessary decisions to defend their people. When they do so, they have the right to expect the unquestioning obedience of everyone (Romans 13:1–5). This allows them to act with the authority of God. Only these governing authorities can declare a 'just war'.

The conditions for a 'just war'

Catholic teaching in the Catechism lays down strict conditions for a war to be declared 'just'. All of these conditions must be met before such a declaration can legitimately be made.

- The damage inflicted by an aggressor on the country, or countries, must be 'lasting, grave and certain'.
- All other means of ending the conflict must have been shown to be 'impractical or ineffective'. Negotiations between the sides must have been tried and seen to have failed.
- The 'just war' must have a serious chance of succeeding.
- The arms and force used during a just war must not be out of all proportion to the force used by the aggressor. This is particularly important at a time when many nations of the world could use nuclear weapons. The important principle here is that of 'proportionality'. Any practice is ruled out that would cause excessive suffering to the enemy. In effect, this means that nuclear, chemical and biological forms of warfare are totally unacceptable in any just war situation. Nothing can justify the devastation that they would cause.
- Only the legitimate government of a country can declare a just war. Even then the normal standards of humanity must be respected. Enemy civilians, wounded soldiers and prisoners of war must be treated with care and respect. They must not be targeted, tortured or mistreated. The mass extermination of a people, nation or an ethnic group (as in 'ethnic cleansing') is a grave sin. Moreover, a person involved in such conduct cannot claim that they were simply carrying out instructions. Each person, in a war, is ultimately responsible to God for his or her own actions.

Extract 1

All citizens and all governments are obliged to work for the avoidance of war. However, as long as the danger of war persists . . . governments cannot be denied the right of lawful self-defence, once all peace efforts have failed.

CCC (2308)

Understanding the principle

The theory of the 'just war' was first formulated by St Augustine of Hippo in the fourth century. He saw war as justified when a neighbour was threatened by the use of force. St Thomas Aquinas (1225–74) was a Dominican friar whose influence on the Catholic Church has been greater than that of anyone except Peter and Paul. He argued that war was justified as long as it was fought in self-defence. Both Augustine and Aquinas believed that the destructive effects of war could be limited if it was fought under certain strict conditions. This is what their teaching set out to achieve. In this sense it had a clear humanitarian aim.

Until the twentieth century the 'just war' theory was largely unchallenged within the main Christian Churches. The only opposition came from pacifist groups such as the Quakers. Opposition in recent times, however, has come from those concerned about the destructiveness of modern warfare. There has also been a concern in many growing modern Christian movements to return to the lifestyle and teachings of the early Christians and especially of Jesus. It is very difficult to support the 'just war' theory by appealing to the New Testament alone.

WORK TO DO

1 Make a list of conditions which would have to be met for a Christian to fight in a 'just war'.

2 Some Roman Catholics believe that it is not wrong for them to kill in a 'just war'. Give three reasons why they might have arrived at this conclusion.

3 a) Do you think that war could ever be justified from a Christian point of view?
   b) If so, how? If not, why not?

4 'War is always wrong. There are no circumstances in which it is "Christian" to kill someone else.' Produce as many arguments as you can for and against this statement.

Extract 2

In this age, which boasts of its atomic power, it no longer makes sense to maintain that war is a fit instrument with which to repair the violation of justice.

Pope John XXIII, Pacem in Terris *(Peace on Earth)*

DISCUSSION POINT

Someone has said that 'The opposition of Christianity to all forms of conflict must rule out any possibility of a just war.' Is this an opinion that you share?

KEY WORDS

Beatitudes
New Testament
Pacificism
Paul
Peter
Quakers

Do you think that this photograph is making an ironic comment on the futility of war and if so, what?

6.3 NUCLEAR WARFARE

KEY QUESTION

How has the development and spread of nuclear weapons necessarily changed the way we look at war?

In 1945 two atomic bombs were dropped on the Japanese cities of Hiroshima and Nagasaki, killing over 140,000 people. Thousands more suffered the appalling after-effects of radiation poisoning for the rest of their lives. Thankfully, this is the only time that nuclear weapons have been actually used in war. Their use brought the Second World War to an abrupt end. The bombs dropped on those two cities were very small by modern standards. They contained an explosive force equivalent to about 13,000 tonnes of dynamite. Modern nuclear weapons can carry an explosive force of more than 10 million tonnes of dynamite. The total nuclear arsenal in the world today is thought to be equivalent to at least 10,000 million tonnes of dynamite, although it may be much larger. No one is sure.

The arms race

At the time of Hiroshima and Nagasaki only the USA had nuclear weapons. It was not long, however, before other countries joined the 'nuclear club'. In 1949 the USSR developed and tested its own nuclear weapons. Soon an arms race developed between the two countries. Within a short time the USA and the USSR were joined as nuclear powers by Britain, France and China. The 'Club' is now much larger. Iran, Israel, South Africa, Egypt, Pakistan, India and North Korea, together with some others, are thought to have a nuclear capability. The basic requirement for a nuclear bomb is plutonium, which is produced by nuclear reactors. Any country which has such reactors to produce energy has the capacity to produce its own nuclear weapons. It is thought that many more countries will have this capacity within the next decade or so.

Some people argue that the arms race is the best guarantee we have of peace. The so-called 'balance of terror' in the world, they argue, means that no country would dare to use nuclear weapons because of the possible consequences. There may be some truth in this argument but at the same time the arms race also:
* risks aggravating the causes of war – injustice, envy, distrust and pride.
* creates considerable danger because the worldwide sales of arms threaten international order.
* creates great inequality by encouraging poor countries to spend immense amounts of money on building up supplies of weapons. Money is squandered on arms when it should be spent on people living without the basic necessities of food and shelter.

The future

The Campaign for Nuclear Disarmament (CND) has argued since the 1950s that the world does not need nuclear weapons. Many Christians agree with this point of view and belong to Christian CND. Most people would like to see the world destroy its nuclear weapons (called 'disarmament') and the call to do so has taken two forms:

Extract 1

Every act of war directed to the indiscriminate destruction of whole cities or vast areas with their inhabitants is a crime against God and man.

Bishops at the Second Vatican Council

Extract 2

Nuclear deterrence has kept the peace for 40 years and a non-nuclear world would be much more dangerous. The temptation for the superpowers to use some of the many nasty conventional chemical or biological weapons at their disposal would be increased . . .

Editorial in The Sunday Times, *19 January 1986*

1 A call for multilateral disarmament This means that everyone who possesses such weapons agrees to disarm at the same time and at the same speed. Pope John XXIII called for multilateral disarmament in his encyclical *Pacem in Terris* (*Peace on Earth*) published in 1963. The Pope argued that the arms race should be ended and all nuclear weapons destroyed (see Extract 2 in 6.2).

2 A call for unilateral disarmament This means that one side with nuclear weapons disarms on its own whilst encouraging others to follow its example. In 1982 unilateral disarmament was supported by a Church of England report called '*The Church and the Bomb*'. The report's recommendation was rejected by the General Synod, the Church's ruling body, which insisted that multilateral disarmament was the only way forward. All Christian Churches agree that a nuclear war is unthinkable – for whatever reason. This means that the theory of the 'just war' seems to have been left behind by events. Remember – a good end (defending one's country) cannot justify immoral means (the use of weapons which kill indiscriminately and threaten the future of the world). That is the teaching of the Catholic Church.

WORK TO DO

1 a) Give one reason why some people argue that Britain should have nuclear weapons.
 b) Give one reason why some people argue that Britain should give up its nuclear weapons.

2 Explain what is meant by these two terms:
 a) unilateral disarmament
 b) multilateral disarmament.

3 Why do most Christians think that nuclear war is wrong?

4 What is the teaching of the Catholic Church on nuclear weapons?

Extract 3

Before the bomb, man had to live with the idea of his death as an individual; from now onwards, mankind has to live with the idea of death as a species.

Arthur Koestler, author

DISCUSSION POINT

Do you think that it would be a good idea, and set an example to other countries, if Britain were to unilaterally disarm?

Some people would say that the dropping of the atomic bombs on Hiroshima and Nagasaki changed for ever the way we look at war. Do you agree?

6.4 PACIFISM

KEY QUESTION

What is pacifism and why is it an attractive position for many Christians to hold?

CONSULT

Matthew 5:9,39

Extract 1

We utterly deny all outward wars and strife, and fightings with outward weapons, for any end, or under any pretence whatsoever; this is our testimony to the whole world. The Spirit of Christ by which we are guided is not changeable, so as once to command us from a thing as evil, and again to move unto it; and we certainly know, and testify to the world that the Spirit of Christ, which leads us into all truth, will never move us to fight and war against any man, neither for the Kingdom of Christ nor for the kingdoms of this world.

Quaker Declaration, 1660

Pacifism is the belief that human beings should always seek a peaceful, non-violent, solution to all forms of conflict. All disputes involving individuals, groups and nations should be solved in a peaceful way. Killing other human beings can never be justified in any circumstances. For its first three centuries members of the Christian Church rarely signed up for service in the Roman Army. They found the teaching of Jesus about violence crystal clear:

- 'Blessed are the peacemakers, for they will be called sons of God' (Matthew 5:9)
- 'Do not resist an evil person. If someone strikes you on the right cheek, turn to him the other also.' (Matthew 5:39).

Things changed, however, when Constantine became Roman Emperor and embraced the Christian faith at the start of the fourth century. When this happened, many Christians felt able to join the Roman armed forces for the first time. The Roman Catholic Church embraced the 'just war' approach and pacifism went out of fashion. It remains so within the official documents and teaching of the Roman Catholic Church. The CCC, for instance, recognises that some provision should be made for 'conscientious objectors' in time of war but insists that they should play a non-combatant role, such as stretcher-bearing. In the First and Second World Wars conscientious objectors often found themselves in the front-line of fighting while carrying out such duties. It was certainly not an easy option.

The Roman Catholic Church does not have a strong tradition of pacifism. Only one Christian group, the Quakers, is openly committed to non-violence and pacifism (see Extract 1). Since they were first established in the seventeenth century Quakers have argued that the only way to bring an end to violence of any kind is to appeal to that part of God which is in everyone – the Inner Voice or Spirit. Their testimony throughout the world has always been that God brings his own love and peace into every situation, no matter what its potential for violence might be.

Christian pacifism

Christians who are pacifists justify their opposition to all forms of violence on the following grounds:
- the commandment which declares 'You shall not kill' (Exodus 13:20). For many Christians this all-embracing prohibition rules out not only war but also any violence directed towards human beings or animals.
- the teaching of Jesus in the Sermon on the Mount (see 1.6 and 1.7). Pacifists point, in particular, to Matthew 5:39,44 and 48. They wonder how these verses can demand anything but a pacifist approach to life.
- the actions and example of Jesus. When Jesus was arrested his disciple, Peter, drew a sword and cut off the ear of the High Priest's servant (Luke 22:51). Jesus healed the man and made it clear that violence was not his chosen path (see Extract 2). He accepted the death that lay ahead of him without question and in so doing set an example for others to follow.
- an evil action can never justify another evil action in retaliation. The teaching of the Bible is that killing is wrong, no matter how strong the provocation might be.

- history shows clearly that war rarely solves any problem. The underlying causes of the war are still there when the conflict ends.

The Biblical case for pacifism is strong. It seems surprising, therefore, that it does not have stronger support in any of the major Churches.

'Put your sword back in its place,' Jesus said to him, 'for all who draw the sword will die by the sword. Do you think I cannot call on my Father, and he will at once put at my disposal more than twelve legions of angels.'

Matthew 26:52–53

Conscientious objectors working as stretcher-bearers in the First World War. Does it surprise you that none of the major Christian Churches adopts a pacifist approach?

WORK TO DO

1 a) What is pacifism?
   b) Explain the term 'non-violent protest', using one Christian example.
   c) 'Jesus didn't teach anything about pacifism.' Do you agree with this comment?

2 'All Christians should be pacifists.' Do you agree?

3 One of the Ten Commandments forbids murder. Some Roman Catholics are pacifists. Give two reasons why they believe that their faith requires them to be pacifists.

4 Imagine a discussion between someone who believed in the just war theory and someone who was a pacifist. What arguments might each of them put forward to support their case?

DISCUSSION POINT

Why do you think that so few Churches support a message of pacifism?

KEY WORDS

Pacifism
Peter
Quakers
Sermon on the Mount

PERSONAL ISSUES AND THE SACRAMENTS

7.1 THE SACRAMENTS

KEY QUESTION

What are sacraments and what difference should they make to the everyday life of a Roman Catholic?

A sacrament has been described as an 'efficacious symbol'. This means that it is a special kind of sign that actually brings about the very thing that it represents. This definition fits both Christ and his Church perfectly:

- Jesus is not just a sign of God's love for us, he *is* that perfect love. Jesus is the living proof that God cares for all his children.
- the Church is also a sacrament. Through the life which the Holy Spirit gives the Church it is an effective sign of God's salvation to the world. It is more, though, than a sacrament. It is the very life of God on earth. The risen Jesus lives and works in the Church which, in turn, works for the establishment of God's kingdom on earth. Through the Church all Catholics are called by God to be sacrament-people – signs to the world of God's presence on earth.

The sacraments are special actions of Christ, entrusted to and working through the Church (see Extract 2). They are effective symbols. More than that, though, they actually bring God's life to those who experience and enjoy their celebration. If they are received properly then they must bear fruit in every believer.

The meaning of the sacraments

The sacraments were described above as 'efficacious'. This means that they are 'capable of having the desired effect'. They are effective because Jesus himself works through them. The power of the sacraments comes from God, not from the priest or the way he dispenses them. The words and the form in which the sacraments are given (the ritual) are of only secondary importance. They have a considerable effect on those who receive them because:

- **the sacraments are signs.** Words and actions in the sacraments bring to us spiritual realities which are way beyond our senses, although they come to us through them. We can see the water poured over a baby's head at baptism; smell the anointing with holy oil; taste the consecrated bread and wine at the Eucharist; and hear as two people exchange their marriage vows with each other. Through each of the sacraments we can celebrate God's friendship with his people, since they bring together, and unite, the divine and the human. This is why the Catholic Church values the sacraments so highly.
- **the sacraments bring God's grace.** Each of the seven sacraments celebrated by the Catholic Church brings God's free, and undeserved, love to anyone open to receive it. It is

Extract 1

The purpose of the sacraments is to sanctify [make holy] men, to build up the Body of Christ and, finally, to give worship to God. Because they are signs they also instruct. They not only pre-suppose faith but by words and objects they also nourish, strengthen and express it. That is why they are called the sacraments of faith.

CCC (1123)

Why do you think that sacraments, if possible, involve the whole Church?

People line up to receive Holy Communion. From where does the spiritual power of the Sacraments come?

God's grace alone that can make us pleasing to him. The Sacrament of Baptism introduces us into God's family whilst the Sacrament of Reconciliation restores our broken relationship with God. All of the sacraments increase and deepen our friendship with God. For Catholics, joining in the sacraments is necessary for salvation. Without the Church, and its sacramental life, there is no salvation.

The sacraments, then, bring God's grace and love to the recipient. Only one condition is needed for them to bear fruit in each believer – they must be received worthily and with thanksgiving to God. Everyone must respond to God in faith even as the sacrament is offered to them. The importance of faith in receiving the sacraments is underlined by the quotation from the CCC in Extract 2. The people who receive in faith must also co-operate with God in the gifts which he gives to them through the sacraments. Through the sacraments God offers his friendship and love. We must respond to them by faith and accept the gift of eternal life which is so generously offered by God.

WORK TO DO

1 Read Extract 2 carefully. This extract from the Catechism explains the difference that the sacraments should make in the life of every Catholic. Write a paragraph explaining just what that difference is.

2 The Roman Catholic Church believes that God's help can be obtained through the sacraments. Do you agree?

3 The sacraments have been described as 'efficacious symbols'.
   a) What do you think this phrase means?
   b) How do you think it applies to the sacraments?
   c) Think about one of the sacraments with which you are familiar. Explain how you would expect someone receiving it to be made different through it.

Extract 2

The sacraments of the New Testament, instituted by Christ the Lord and entrusted to the Church, as they are actions of Christ and the Church, stand out as the signs and means by which the faith is expressed and strengthened, worship is rendered to God and the sanctification [making holy] of humankind is effected . . .

The Code of Canon Law

DISCUSSION POINT

Do you agree that the sacraments are so very important because, without them, we could know or experience little of God?

KEY WORDS

Baptism
Eucharist
Holy Spirit
New Testament
Priest
Sacrament

7.2 THE SACRAMENTS OF INITIATION

KEY QUESTION

What are the three Sacraments of Initiation and what are the links between them?

As the CCC points out, there was a long stage of preparation in the early Church before a person was admitted into full membership. This full membership came through the celebration of the three Sacraments of Initiation: Baptism, Confirmation and the Mass or Eucharist. In the early Church these three sacraments were usually administered to adults at the single service – the Easter Vigil. By the third century, however, churches were being built with their own baptisteries. Candidates were plunged naked into the water and called 'newborn' as they emerged. They wore a white garment from Easter to Whitsun and were anointed with 'chrism' (oil) before receiving the body and blood of Christ at their first Communion. Everyone felt that the new converts were following the example of Jesus by submitting themselves to such baptism.

Towards infant baptism

By the Middle Ages the Catholic Church had committed itself to baptising babies rather than adults. The main reason for this was that illness and plague caused a very high infant mortality rate in almost all families. The Church clearly taught that baptism was necessary for certain salvation. Unbaptised people, including babies, could not enter heaven and so parents wanted their children baptised as soon as possible. As young babies could not indicate their own commitment to Christ the responsibility was taken over by parents and the Church community, represented by godparents. The same responsibility is expressed through the service of infant baptism today (see 7.3).

Baptism and confirmation

The Orthodox Church separated from the Catholic Church at the Great Schism of 1054. By this time there was a marked difference in approach to the three sacraments of initiation between the two Churches. This difference remains with us today. The Catholic Church baptises babies and then allows time to elapse before accepting the person for Confirmation. Confirmation draws a person back to 'confirm' for themselves, in front of the Church, the vows that others made on their behalf when they were baptised. Obviously, not everyone who has been baptised is confirmed. Confirmation involves a high level of commitment to the Christian way of life. Inevitably this must have a marked effect on the way that a person lives. Confirmation is only meaningful if this commitment is present. It is the commitment, rather than the ritual and anointing, which makes the sacrament important.

The Orthodox Church, in its service of Chrismation, combines the baptism of infants with their confirmation and the taking of first communion. All three take place at the same time.

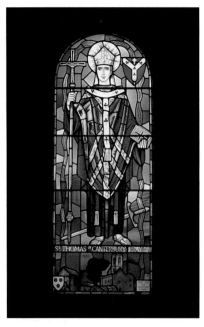

Of the three sacraments of initiation only confirmation is usually performed by a bishop. Can you find out why?

Adult baptism

The Second Vatican Council encouraged the Catholic Church to look again at the possibility of baptising adults, without in any way questioning the validity of infant baptism. Adult baptism, it insisted, was spiritually valid and important. The 'Rite of Christian Initiation of Adults' (RCIA) contains four periods and three stages for adult baptism. These take the seeker from the precatechuminate (earliest) stages of inquiring into the Catholic faith to the 'Rite of Initiation' when they take the bread and wine of the Mass for the first time. As in the early Church the period of initiation ends on Pentecost Sunday.

WORK TO DO

1 In the early centuries of the Catholic Church:
   a) What were the sacraments of initiation?
   b) When were the sacraments of initiation usually administered?
   c) When were the converts to the faith called 'newborn'?

2 a) Why do you think that the early Church insisted on a long period of instruction before baptism?
   b) How is the Catholic Church trying to restore this tradition today?

3 a) What do you think was the symbolism behind early converts being plunged naked into the waters of baptism?
   b) Why do you think that these converts wore white clothes from Easter to Whitsun?

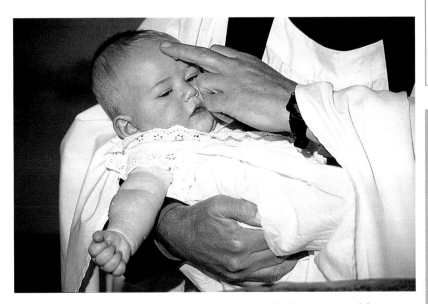

A baby is anointed by a priest. What responsibility is carried by parents and godparents in the service of infant baptism?

Extract 1

The Sacraments of Christian Initiation – Baptism, Confirmation and the Eucharist – lay the foundations of every Christian life . . . The faithful are born anew by Baptism, strengthened by the sacrament of Confirmation, and receive in the Eucharist the food of eternal life. By means of these sacraments of Christian initiation, they thus receive in increasing measures the treasures of the divine life and advance towards the perfection of charity.

CCC (1212)

DISCUSSION POINT

Do you think that the Church should make wider use of adult baptism as the Second Vatican Council suggested?

KEY WORDS

Baptism
Chrism
Chrismation
Confirmation
Easter Vigil
Easter Whitsun
Eucharist
mass
Orthodox Church
Sacrament
Second Vatican Council

7.3 INFANT BAPTISM

KEY QUESTION

What is baptism and why do Catholic parents want to have their children baptised?

CONSULT

Romans 6:4;
Colossians 2:12;
John 1:9; Ephesians 5:8

Extract 1

God is our Father (Abba);
Jesus is our brother,
The Holy Spirit lives within us.

From the baptismal service

Extract 2

I tell you the truth, no one can enter the kingdom of God unless he is born of water and the Spirit.

John 3:5

Extract 3

... go and make disciples of all nations, baptising them in the name of the Father and of the Son of the Holy Spirit, and teaching them to obey everything I have commanded you.

Matthew 28:19,20

Baptism is the first sacrament that a person receives in the Catholic Church and it opens the door to all the others. The sacrament is linked with the death and resurrection of Jesus because each recipient symbolically dies with Christ before entering into the new life and mystery of his resurrection. Baptism initiates each person into the Church, the Body of Christ. Through baptism Original Sin is forgiven and the support of the Christian community is extended so that a person can live a Christian life. It marks the rebirth of every recipient as a child of light who is able to bring the light of Christ into the world.

The rite of baptism

The priest presides over the service of Infant Baptism, representing both God and the whole Christian family, the Church. The service itself usually, although not always, takes the form of a Mass. The important thing is that the sacrament of baptism should always be celebrated in an assembly of Christian believers. There are several distinct stages to the service.

1 The priest asks the parents for the child's name. To call a child by his or her name underlines the uniqueness of each individual before God. The tradition is that one of the child's names should be that of a saint to underline the Catholic belief in the 'Communion of Saints'.

2 The parents and godparents are asked questions to determine the depth of their own religious faith. One of the godparents must be an active, fully initiated Roman Catholic. Godparents and the worshipping community promise to help the parents to bring up the child in the Catholic faith. The priest welcomes the child into the Catholic family: '(Name), the Christian community welcomes you with great joy. In its name I claim you for Christ our Saviour by the sign of his cross. I now trace the cross on your forehead and invite your parents and godparents to do the same.'

3 The Liturgy of the Word follows. If the baptism takes place on a Sunday, or an important feast day, the readings are taken from the Lectionary. Passages will be from the Old Testament, the Epistles and the Gospels.

4 The baby is anointed with oil of catechumens to symbolise the healing of God and to ward off evil. The priest reinforces this by laying his hands on the child whilst calling down God's blessing. Then, after the water has been blessed, the priest baptises the baby 'in the name of the Father, and of the Son and of the Holy Spirit'. Finally the baby is anointed with chrism; the parents are given a candle lit from the Paschal Candle; a new white shawl is placed around the child and the family is blessed by the priest.

The symbols of baptism

Four symbols play an important role in the service.

- **Water**   To baptise means to immerse or plunge into water. Water symbolises new life, cleansing and death. Baptismal water indicates death to the old life and a share in the new, resurrection life of Christ. The child's original sin is washed away. The new child of God shares in his eternal life.
- **Oil**   Oil heals and protects and is a sign of being set aside or chosen by God to perform a special task. The oil shows that the baby has been Christened (Christ = the Anointed One).
- **Light**   The candle handed to the child's parents is a challenge to carry the light of Christ into a dark world. If others are to see Christ in the world it will only be through the lives of those who love him.
- **The white garment**   The early Christians put on white clothes as they came out of the baptismal pool. Such clothes showed that Christ had cleansed their sins. The white garment placed around the child today indicates the same thing.

What does this stained-glass window show Jesus receiving at his baptism?

WORK TO DO

1 Explain:
   a) the symbolic importance of water in the service of Infant Baptism
   b) why a candle is handed to the child's parents during the sacrament of Infant Baptism
   c) why a child is anointed with oil at baptism
   d) why a white shawl is placed around the baby after it has been baptised.

2 Explain the responsibilities that parents and godparents accept for the child who is being baptised.

3 'There is little point in baptising babies when they do not understand what is going on.' Do you agree with this opinion?

What is the symbolic importance of the white clothes that this baby is wearing for her baptism?

DISCUSSION POINT

If you have children in future years, what do you think infant baptism will mean to you?

KEY WORDS

Baptism
Chrism
Communion of Saints
Epistles
Gospels
Holy Spirit
Infant Baptism
Lectionary
Liturgy of the Word
Mass
Old Testament
Original Sin
Paschal Candle
Sacrament
Saint
Sunday

KEY QUESTION

What lies at the heart of the service of Confirmation and what effect does it have upon the believer?

CONSULT

Acts 8:16,17

Extract 1

When they arrived, they prayed for them that they might receive the Holy Spirit, because the Holy Spirit had not yet come upon any of them; they had simply been baptised into the name of Jesus. Then Peter and John placed their hands on them, and they received the Holy Spirit.

Acts 8:16,17

Extract 2

All-powerful God, Father of our Lord Jesus Christ, by water and the Holy Spirit, you freed your sons and daughters from sin, and gave them new life. Send your Holy Spirit upon them to be their helper and guide. Give them the spirit of wisdom and understanding, the spirit of right judgement and courage, the spirit of knowledge and reverence. Fill them with the spirit of wonder and awe in your presence. We ask this through Christ our Lord. Amen.

A prayer said by the bishop at Confirmation

Confirmation is one of the three Sacraments of Initiation into the Christian Church, along with Baptism and the Eucharist (see 7.2). It brings to a conclusion the spiritual process that began with baptism. It is the seal of baptism, a receiving of the Holy Spirit, a confirming of the promises made on the child's behalf at Baptism. Adult converts are usually confirmed at the Easter Vigil immediately after their baptism. Young people are confirmed several years after they are baptised. In some dioceses, children are confirmed when they are as young as six years old but usually the Sacrament is performed when they are in their early teens.

Confirmation

Confirmation takes place during a service which stresses the links between the different Sacraments of Initiation. The sacrament is usually performed by the bishop, so underlining the importance that the Church attaches to it (although the parish priest can perform the ceremony). Confirmation takes place with the Mass and is performed after the Liturgy of the Word has been completed. Those being confirmed are asked to renew their baptismal promises. Their own faith is confirmed by saying the Apostles' Creed.

The bishop, and any priests concelebrating the service, lay their hands on the head of each confirmation candidate. As you can see from Extract 1 the 'laying on of hands' is a practice going back to the apostles and is a way of passing on the Holy Spirit. The bishop traces the sign of the cross on the forehead with 'chrism' (oil) as he says: '(Name), be sealed with the gift of the Holy Spirit'. The chrism – a mixture of olive oil and perfume blessed by the bishop on Holy Thursday – is a reminder that the goodness of the confirmed should spread through the world. Oil is a sign of healing, holiness and strength, as well as a sign of being sealed with God's Spirit to live out the roles of priest, prophet and king. These are the same roles that Jesus himself carried out on earth. Anointing with the sign of the cross underlines how each Christian must follow in the footsteps of Jesus and witness boldly to those around him. The bishop also lightly slaps the face of each candidate with two fingers. This is a symbolic gesture to show the suffering and persecution which the person may have to undergo for their faith in the future.

The Peace, the Prayers of the Faithful and the Lord's Prayer all follow. Each candidate takes Holy Communion as a symbol of their unity with God and with each other. Sharing in communion at this moment brings together the three Sacraments of Initiation.

The effects of confirmation

The Catechism links Confirmation with the gift of the Holy Spirit to the disciples at Pentecost. The CCC (1303) explains that confirmation grants five special graces to each recipient:

1 Confirmation completes our sonship in God, by which we can say 'Abba, Father' (Romans 8:15).

2 Confirmation makes us more deeply one with Christ.

3 Confirmation helps us to grow in the gifts of the Holy Spirit.

4 Confirmation links us more closely with the Church.

5 Confirmation gives us strength (confirms us) to witness to our faith in Christ.

WORK TO DO

1 How are baptism and confirmation linked together?

2 Explain the meaning of the following actions used in confirmation:
   a) the laying on of hands
   b) the anointing with chrism.

3 Do you think that being confirmed is likely to make a person a better Christian? Explain your answer carefully.

4 Choose two symbols or symbolic actions used in the sacrament of Confirmation. For each of them explain how it might help the person being confirmed to feel God's presence with them.

KEY WORDS

Apostles' Creed
Baptism
Bishop
Chrism
Confirmation
Easter Vigil
Eucharist
Holy Communion
Holy Spirit
Lord's Prayer
Mass
Pentecost
Priest
Sacrament
Sign of peace
Sign of the cross

DISCUSSION POINT

What did your Confirmation mean to you?

Why do you think that Confirmation is usually carried out by the area bishop?

Why do you think that the 'laying on of hands' is such an important part of the Confirmation service?

7.5 THE EUCHARIST

KEY QUESTION

How did Jesus use his last meal with his disciples to give them, and the Church, the most important sacrament?

CONSULT

Luke 22:7–23

Extract 1

. . . we know ourselves to be bound by the command the Lord gave on the eve of his Passion: 'Do this in remembrance of me'. We carry out this command of the Lord by celebrating the memorial of his sacrifice. In so doing, we offer to the Father what he has given to us: the gifts of his creation, bread and wine which, by the power of the Holy Spirit and by the words of Christ, have become the body and blood of Christ. Christ is thus really and mysteriously made present.

CCC (1356, 1357)

Extract 2

Those who have been raised to the dignity of the royal priesthood by Baptism, and configured more deeply to Christ by Confirmation, participate with the whole community in the Lord's own sacrifice by means of the Eucharist.

CCC (1322)

The Eucharist (the Mass) is the greatest sacrament of the Roman Catholic Church. Whilst Baptism and Confirmation, the other Sacraments of Initiation, can only be celebrated once in a person's life, Catholics are encouraged to take Holy Communion as often as possible. In a real sense it begins where the other two leave off, since a person's first Communion is taken after they have been confirmed. Properly taken, and understood, it will provide them with spiritual nourishment for the rest of their lives.

The Jewish Passover

The necessary background to understanding the Eucharist lies in the Jewish festival of Passover. This festival, celebrated by Jews for centuries down to the present day, retells the events of the Exodus – the release by the Egyptian Pharaoh of his Jewish slaves. Before God brought the final plague upon him, the Jews were told to sprinkle the blood of a lamb on the lintel and doorposts of their home. The Angel of Death then 'passed over' all of the buildings marked in this way but killed the eldest son in every Egyptian home. It was the blood of the lamb that saved the Jews.

Each year, at the Passover meal, Jewish parents retell this story to their children and in this way the memory of the ancient event is kept alive. During the retelling everyone acts as if they had been present at the actual event. They share, through the different kinds of food on the table, the bitterness of slavery and the intervention of God to rescue their ancestors.

The Last Supper

When Jesus met with his disciples at the Last Supper it was to share with them a traditional Passover meal. The unleavened bread and goblets of wine were there on the table in front of them. Jesus, though, was to use these traditional Passover symbols to teach his disciples an unforgettable lesson – the meaning of his imminent death. The bread and the wine were to be the central symbols for the Eucharist which was to become, in the hands of the Church, the centre of all its worship. During his meal with his disciples Jesus took the unleavened bread, blessed it and broke it in front of them saying: 'Take and eat; this is my body'. At the Passover meal everybody eats unleavened bread as a reminder of the haste with which the Jews left Egypt under the leadership of Moses. They didn't even have time to let the bread that they were baking rise. For Jesus the bread was a symbol of his own body, soon to be broken on a Roman cross.

Jesus then took the Passover goblet of wine, a symbol of joy shared among friends, and told them: 'Drink from it, all of you. This is my blood of the covenant, which is poured out for many for the forgiveness of sins' (Matthew 26: 26–35). The symbol of wine became a symbol of sorrow. Just as the lamb of old was sacrificed to save the Jews, so Jesus, the Lamb of God, was sacrificed on the cross to save all who believe in him. The wine is a symbol of that sacrifice. To Roman Catholics the Mass is a sacrifice. This is why, in the Mass, Jesus is called 'the Lamb of God'.

Roman Catholics believe in the 'Real Presence' of Jesus each time the Mass is celebrated. This is the major difference between the Roman Catholic Church and the different Protestant Churches. As the CCC says (see Extract 1), the gifts of God's creation, bread and wine, become the actual broken body and shed blood of Jesus at their consecration in the Mass. It goes on to say that we must consider the Eucharist as:

- an act of thanksgiving and praise to God, the Father

- the sacrificial memorial of Christ and his Body

- the presence of Christ by the power of his word and his Spirit.

What did the symbols of bread and wine become in the hands of Jesus?

WORK TO DO

1 What is the difference between the Eucharist and the other Sacraments of Initiation, Baptism and Confirmation?

2 a) What is the Passover?
   b) Why is this festival called the Passover?
   c) What is the Exodus?

3 a) What kind of meal was the Last Supper?
   b) Why did they eat unleavened bread at the Passover?
   c) What use did Jesus make of the bread on the table?
   d) What use did Jesus make of the wine on the table?

DISCUSSION POINT

Why do you think that the Eucharist is at the heart of worship for most Christians – and especially for Roman Catholics?

KEY WORDS

Baptism
Confirmation
Disciple
Eucharist
Holy Communion
Last Supper
Mass
Moses
Passover
Protestant
Sacrament

The last meal that Jesus shared with his disciples was a Passover meal. What was the link between that meal and the Jewish festival?

7.6 THE LITURGY OF THE WORD

KEY QUESTION

What is the Liturgy of the Word and why is it an important part of the Mass?

CONSULT

Corinthians 11:17–34

Extract 1

Christians come together in one place for the Eucharistic assembly. At its head is Christ himself, the principal agent of the Eucharist. He is the high priest of the New Covenant; it is he himself who presides invisibly over every Eucharistic celebration. It is in representing him that the bishop or priest acting in the person of Christ the head . . . presides over the assembly, speaks after the readings, receives the offerings, and says the Eucharistic Prayer.

CCC (1348)

At the Last Supper Jesus transformed the unleavened bread that was on the table for the Passover meal into his body, shortly to be broken on the cross. Bread is a universal symbol of life. The eucharistic bread – the body of Christ – is the spiritual food necessary for the life of the spirit. The spirit can only be nourished by frequent participation in the Eucharist. Jesus also transformed the wine into his blood. In the Old Testament wine is a symbol of joy and happiness (Psalm 104:13–15). By turning the wine into his blood, Jesus made it the symbol of his sacrificial death on the cross. The sacrifice of Jesus gives us eternal life and friendship with God, the Father.

The liturgy of the Mass falls into two parts – the Liturgy of the Word and the Liturgy of the Eucharist. The Liturgy of the Word has its origins in the old synagogue services which brought people together to pray, read, study and learn from God's Word, the Jewish Scriptures. The Liturgy of the Eucharist reflects the Jewish Temple service in which people gathered to pray and offer sacrifice. It also has its roots in the Jewish Passover meal.

The Liturgy of the Word

The whole of the Mass is one single act of worship. After an opening greeting from the priest to the people (see Extract 1), the Mass begins with a procession in which the Lectionary, the book containing God's word, is held high. The priest, acting in the person of Christ (see Extracts 1 and 2), processes to the altar with the other ministers. The priest kisses the altar as a sign of respect and love for Jesus. The Lectionary is placed on the lectern. In the Penitential Rite which follows, the priest and the people acknowledge their sinfulness before God and seek his forgiveness. The Gloria ('Glory to God') is recited or sung, praising the Trinity before the prayer for that day is offered.

The Liturgy of the Word falls into six divisions.
1 The first reading and the responsorial Psalm. This reading is usually from the Old Testament. The response, from one of the Psalms, expresses the willingness of the congregation to take God's word to their hearts.

2 The second reading comes from one of the Epistles and is followed by the Alleluia verse, which is an expression of willingness to listen to the God who speaks through his word.

3 The key reading in the Liturgy of the Word comes from one of the Gospels and is read by the priest. The people show their reverence for the Gospel by standing and marking themselves with the sign of the cross. In this way the people are showing their willingness to make God's word come alive in their lives by what they think, say and do.

4 The homily. The priest or deacon explores a theme from the readings and shows the people how to live a better Christian life.

5 The Creed. The Church community expresses its joint faith by reciting together the Nicene Creed, a statement of Catholic faith. This traditional statement of faith binds the living community of the Church even closer together and links them to the Communion of Saints in past ages. The faith of the Church is unchanged and unchanging.

6 General Intercessions (the Bidding Prayers). The people pray with confidence that God will answer their prayers for the world, the Church and each other.

WORK TO DO

1 a) Into which two parts does the Roman Catholic Mass fall?
   b) Where are the origins of the Liturgy of the Word to be found?
   c) Where are the origins of the Liturgy of the Eucharist to be found?

2 Explain what is meant by the 'Liturgy of the Word'.

3 Read the quotations in Extracts 1 and 2. Explain, in your own words:
   a) the importance of Christ in the Mass
   b) the role played by the priest in the Mass.

DISCUSSION POINT

Why do you think that the readings from the Bible, at the heart of the Liturgy of the Word, are so important for all Catholics?

Extract 2

The ministerial priest, by the sacred power he enjoys, moulds and rules the priestly people. Acting in the person of Christ, he brings about the Eucharistic sacrifice, and offers it to God in the name of all the people. For their part, the faithful join in the offering of the Eucharist by virtue of their royal priesthood.

The Second Vatican Council

KEY WORDS

Altar
Communion of Saints
Creed
Epistle
Eucharist
Gloria
Gospel
Homily
Last Supper
Lectern
Lectionary
Liturgy of the Eucharist
Liturgy of the Word
Mass
Nicene Creed
Passover
Priest
Psalm
Sign of the Cross
Synagogue
Temple
Trinity

How is Christ present each time that the Mass is celebrated in a Catholic Church?

7.7 THE LITURGY OF THE EUCHARIST

KEY QUESTION

What happens during the Liturgy of the Eucharist?

Extract 1

Those who are well off, and who are willing, give as each chooses. What is gathered is given to him who presides to assist orphans and widows, those whom illness or any other cause has deprived of resources, prisoners, immigrants and, in a word, all who are in need.

St Justin, second-century Church leader

Extract 2

He is the true and eternal priest who establishes this unending sacrifice. He offered himself as a victim for our deliverance and taught us to make this offering in his memory. As we eat his body which he gave for us, we grow in strength. As we drink his blood which is poured out for us, we are washed clean.

Preface of the Holy Eucharist

The Liturgy of the Eucharist begins with members of the congregation bringing the people's offerings of bread, wine and gifts for the poor to the altar. The Mass is the people's offering to God and, since the symbols of bread and wine show God's goodness to us, it is right that they are offered back to God. The bringing of gifts for the poor has been part of the Eucharist celebration from its earliest days (see Extract 1). The custom is inspired by the example of Jesus, who became poor so that all who believe in him might become rich. The priest prays over the gifts after washing his hands and asking that the forthcoming sacrifice might be acceptable to God.

The Eucharistic Prayer

The Eucharistic Prayer, also called the 'canon of the Mass', is at the heart of the Eucharist. The prayer begins with the 'preface', a prayer which reminds everyone of their duty to thank God through Jesus Christ in the power of the Holy Spirit. The congregation show their assent to the preface by singing or reciting the great hymn of praise, the Sanctus, or the 'Holy, Holy, Holy'.

Then follows the Consecration. This is the moment when the bread and wine are changed into the body and blood of Jesus. In 1551 the Council of Trent asserted that in the Eucharist 'Bread and wine are changed, converted into the body and blood of Christ', before adding 'which conversion the Catholic Church most fittingly calls transubstantiation'. The Church uses four Eucharistic Prayers at different times in the liturgical year and they all:

- call upon the power of the Holy Spirit
- recount the words spoken by Jesus at the Last Supper; acknowledge the saving deeds of Jesus and offer the sacrifice of Jesus to God, the Father
- ask God's blessing on the Church, the living and the dead, and the saints from all ages
- end with the Great Amen, where the whole community responds to all that has been said with a resounding 'yes'.

The communion rite

The people prepare themselves to receive Christ by saying the Lord's Prayer together and offering each other the Sign of Peace. These words and actions confirm each believer in the unity that they share together in Christ. They pray together the Agnus Dei (Lamb of God), recognising their own sinfulness and their need of the healing touch of Jesus as the priest breaks the consecrated host and places a piece of it into the consecrated wine in the chalice. After taking the elements himself the priest shares them with the congregation at the altar. A short time is then spent in silent meditation or in the gentle singing of a psalm or a hymn of praise. The Mass ends when the bishop, priest or deacon blesses and dismisses the people. The words that are used remind everyone of the blessing of the Mass – peace. It also encourages everyone to go out into the community to love others and serve the Lord.

The importance of the Mass

St Thomas Aquinas taught that the Eucharist does for the spiritual life what food does for the body. It helps us to grow and brings great joy. The Eucharist cleanses us from our past sins and preserves us from committing future sin. It develops the gifts of the Holy Spirit – faith, hope and love – in us. The Eucharist gives us the spiritual energy we need to complete our earthly pilgrimage, grants us an insight into what heaven is like and unites us with the 'Church Triumphant' – Mary and the saints in heaven. In short, the Eucharist puts us into contact with the saving effects of the paschal mystery, the eternal life that the sacrifice of Jesus has brought within our reach.

WORK TO DO

1 Read Extract 2. It contains the Preface of the Holy Eucharist. This Preface mentions two spiritual blessings which come to all those who share in the Eucharist. What are they?

2 a) Why do you think that the Mass ends with the people being sent out into the world to serve God?
   b) How do you think that celebrating the Mass might help them to do this better?

3 a) Describe what happens during the Mass.
   b) What link is there between the Mass and living the Christian life day by day?

DISCUSSION POINT

Is it surprising that the issue of what happens to the bread and the wine at the Mass should have become such a divisive issue among Christians?

What is transubstantiation?

Why do you think that the priest takes the elements first before sharing them with members of the congregation?

7.8 SIN AND FORGIVENESS

KEY QUESTION

What does the Catholic Church teach about sin and forgiveness?

Extract 1

Adam and Eve transmitted to their descendants human nature wounded by their own first sin and hence deprived them of original holiness and justice . . .

CCC (414)

Extract 2

Forgive us our debts; as we have also forgiven our debtors . . . For if you forgive men when they sin against you, your heavenly Father will also forgive you. But if you do not forgive men their sins, your Father will not forgive your sins.

Matthew 6:12,14

Extract 3

If you forgive anyone his sins, they are forgiven; if you do not forgive them they are not forgiven.

John 20:24

The Roman Catholic Church has always recognised that sin takes one of two forms:

1 Original sin   The description of the fall of the first man and woman into sin in the Garden of Eden, described in Genesis 3, uses: 'figurative language, but affirms a primeval event' (CCC 390). The Fall, as this event is called, took place at the very beginning of human history. It cannot be dated but it is essential to see it as an actual historical event.

The Scriptures teach that the whole of human history has been affected by the consequences of that first act of human disobedience against God. In the beginning God created man in his own image and everything was perfect. Through the Fall that perfection was lost for ever. The first parents passed on the tendency to sin to all of their descendants. Roman Catholics call this tendency 'concupiscence'. The taint of original sin is forgiven through baptism but this cannot remove the tendency itself. That is where the Sacrament of Reconciliation (see 7.10) and penance become so important.

2 Mortal and venial sins   These terms refer to actual sins committed. In Catholic tradition these actual sins have always been divided into:

- **Mortal sin**   This is sin which involves a radical rupture in the relationship between God and the individual because of the seriousness of the action. For a sin to be mortal the subject matter must be extremely serious; the person must have had a full knowledge of what they were doing and the sin must have been committed willingly. A mortal sin is so serious that it brings death to the soul. For any hope of final forgiveness from such a sin there must be a full, and frank, confession of the sin. Jesus himself recognised that there was a sin, the sin against the Holy Spirit, for which there could be no forgiveness (Matthew 12:31; Mark 3–29; Luke 12:10) but the exact nature of this sin is a matter of continuing theological debate.

- **Venial sin**   This is a moral transgression which is not considered serious enough to break the relationship between God and the sinner. Pardon (venia in Latin) is therefore relatively easy. The New Testament itself seems to draw some kind of distinction between sins which are serious and those which are not. It speaks, for instance, of the gnat and the camel (Matthew 23:24), the speck and the log (Matthew 7:3), the sins that occur in everyday life for which a person will have to give account on the Day of Judgement (Matthew 12:36), and the actions that exclude a person from the Church – and God's kingdom (1 Corinthians 6:9–10).

Forgiveness

Sin inevitably separates God and man. Forgiveness restores a person's broken relationship with God – and others. In the Catholic tradition forgiveness is the sinner's acceptance of the unconditional grace and love extended to them through Jesus Christ and the giving of that forgiveness freely to others. The Lord's Prayer makes it clear that a person's forgiveness by God depends on their own willingness to forgive others (Luke 11:1–4; Matthew 6:9–15). We must be prepared to forgive others as often as we are asked (Matthew 18:21–35). There is no limit to be placed on true forgiveness – God's or ours.

Within the Catholic Church penance, almsgiving and even separation from the Church for a time have been used over the centuries to bring about repentance and forgiveness. Forgiveness is celebrated in the sacraments of Baptism and the Eucharist as well as in that of Reconciliation. For forgiveness to be offered in the Sacrament of Reconciliation there has to be a confession of the sin; sorrow (contrition) and absolution from the priest. You will find out more about this in 7.10. First, though, it is necessary to look more closely at the attitude of Jesus towards forgiveness (see 7.9).

WORK TO DO

1 a) What is Original Sin?
   b) What was the Fall?
   c) What have been the consequences of the Fall?
   d) What is concupiscence?
   e) What is the link between Original Sin and baptism?

2 a) What is a mortal sin?
   b) Is there any hope of forgiveness for the person who has committed a mortal sin?
   c) What is a venial sin?
   d) What must precede the forgiveness of a venial sin?

3 Look at Extracts 2 and 3. What do these quotations suggest about the link between a person being forgiven by God and the willingness of that person to forgive others?

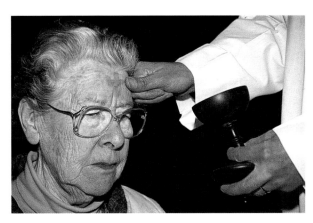

Find out what is happening to this woman on Ash Wednesday and what the link is between this action, sin and forgiveness.

What does the Catholic Church believe about the sinful nature of this young child?

DISCUSSION POINT

Why do you think that Jesus made our forgiveness by God dependent on our willingness to forgive others who have injured us?

KEY WORDS

Absolution
Almsgiving
Baptism
Eucharist
Fall
Holy Spirit
Lord's Prayer
Mortal sin
New Testament
Penance
Venial sin

7.9 JESUS AND FORGIVENESS

KEY QUESTION

What can we learn from the parable of the forgiving father about the attitude of Jesus towards forgiveness?

CONSULT

Mark 2:1–12;
Luke 15:11–32

What is the link between the death of Jesus on the cross and the forgiveness of sins?

The theme of forgiveness is at the centre of the Gospels. John the Baptist came preaching a 'baptism of repentance for the forgiveness of sins' (Mark 1:4). John was preaching the imminent coming of God's kingdom and Jesus made it clear that this promise was fulfilled by his own coming. At the heart of his own work was the forgiveness of humankind (Mark 10:45; Luke 4:18–21). Jesus himself forgave sins (Mark 2:1–12) and, after his death, his disciples offered forgiveness to those who repented of their sins (Acts 5:31). This forgiveness was closely associated with his death on the cross (Mark 10:45). As the Lamb of God, Jesus takes away the sins of the world, as John the Baptist himself recognised (John 1:29).

Forgiveness

Here are two examples of forgiveness from the Gospels – one a miracle and the other a parable.

1 The miracle – Jesus heals a paralysed man (Mark 2:1–12)   This is the only place in Mark's Gospel where Jesus claims to have the authority to forgive sins. The basic argument of the scribes, who had already been compared unfavourably with Jesus (Mark 1:22), was that no one could forgive sins except God. A dispute arose because Jesus told the paralysed man who was brought to him to find healing that his sins were forgiven. When the scribes objected to Jesus implying that he could forgive sins Jesus put a question to them: 'Which is easier: to say to the paralytic, "Your sins are forgiven" or to say "Get up, take your mat and walk"?' (Mark 2:9). Jesus then carried out the more difficult task (healing the paralysed man) to show that he could also meet the easier challenge (forgiving sins). As Jesus said: 'I will prove to you, then, that the Son of Man has authority on earth to forgive sins.' (Mark 2:10).

2 The parable – the forgiving father (Luke 15:11–32)   This parable is the last of three that Luke brought together to illustrate the importance of finding things that had been lost – the lost sheep (Luke 15:1–7); the lost coin (Luke 15:8–10) and the lost son. Jesus told the parable after the Pharisees and others had criticised him for suggesting that the kingdom of God was open to everyone, including sinners and outcasts. They wanted to reserve it for religious people alone. In the story the younger son collects his share of the family inheritance and leaves home. Whilst away he spends all his money on having a good time but when his money runs out his friends desert him. When famine comes he is forced to eat the same food as the pigs that he looks after.

The son decides to return home. His father sees him in the distance and runs to meet him. Overjoyed at seeing his son again, his father gives him clothes, shoes and a ring. The best robe was a sign of honour, the ring a sign of authority and the shoes a sign of a free man (slaves went barefoot). The son is given the best treatment and is not treated like a slave, which was the best he could really have hoped for. The older brother, though, is jealous and self-righteous. Although his father tries to express his love for him this is rejected. He prefers to remain outside the party that his father throws for his brother to express his disgust at what the younger man has done and the welcome that he has been given by his father.

This parable provides a beautiful way of illustrating forgiveness, as well as offering valuable insights which are incorporated in the Sacrament of Reconciliation (see 7.10). In the sacrament forgiveness begins only after the person has decided to express their sorrow at their own sinfulness, just as the younger son does in the parable. The response of the father – a figure who symbolises God – is to welcome his wayward son without any reservations. Similarly, God receives the sinner after they have shown heartfelt contrition. In the sacrament this point is reached when the priest pronounces God's absolution. If necessary the son was prepared to work as a slave for his father to show his genuine repentance, and penance provides the opportunity for the sinner to walk down this path.

WORK TO DO

1 Jesus taught that people should be ready to forgive anyone who had hurt or offended them.
 a) Describe one miracle in which Jesus forgave someone as part of the miracle of healing their body.
 b) Describe one parable in which Jesus taught the meaning of forgiveness.

2 Explain how the parable of the forgiving father might be used to show the attitude of Jesus towards forgiveness.

3 Read the Sermon on the Mount in Matthew 5–7. Refresh your memory by looking back to sections 1.4 and 1.5.
 a) Make a list of the different things that Jesus said in the Sermon about forgiveness.
 b) Do you think a Christian could follow this teaching in their everyday lives today?

DISCUSSION POINT

In the parable of the forgiving father where do your sympathies lie – with the younger son, the elder son, or even with the father?

Extract 1

[This sacrament] is called the sacrament of conversion because it makes sacramentally present Jesus' call to conversion, the first step in returning to the Father from whom one has strayed by sin . . . Jesus calls to conversion. This call is an essential part of the proclamation of the kingdom – Christ's call to conversion continues to resound in the lives of Christians.

CCC (1423, 1427, 1428)

KEY WORDS

Disciple
Gospel
John the Baptist
Miracle
Parable
Penance
Son of Man

The paralysed man is let down through the roof to the feet of Jesus. What did Jesus suggest was the link between the illness of the man and the forgiveness of his sins?

7.10 THE SACRAMENT OF RECONCILIATION

KEY QUESTION

What is the Sacrament of Reconciliation?

Extract 1

I will give you the keys of the kingdom of heaven; whatever you bind on earth will be bound in heaven, and whatever you loose on earth will be loosed in heaven.

Matthew 16:19

Extract 2

If we claim to be without sin, we deceive ourselves and the truth is not in us.

1 John 1:8

Extract 3

Those who are reconciled with God in the sacrament of Penance, experience peace and serenity of conscience, joined to a great consolation of soul because they rise again from their sins to rejoice in God's friendship with the sunshine of the soul that it brings. They are also re-established in the family of the Church rejoicing together with him.

CCC (1468)

Two effects of baptism are the forgiveness of sin and the inclusion of the baptised in the family of God. The Holy Spirit first given in Baptism and Confirmation and continually received through the Eucharist, continues the work of 'conversion' throughout a person's life (see Extract 1 in 7.9). Despite this, though, nothing can take away the human inclination to sin (concupiscence) and so each Catholic needs the Sacrament of Reconciliation.

The new Rite of Reconciliation

Although the sacrament has been practised by the Church for centuries it was given a new focus by the Second Vatican Council. The Council declared that the purpose of penance, or reconciliation as it is now called, is for the sinner to receive God's forgiveness and to be '. . . reconciled with the Church whom [sinners] have wounded by their sin, and who, by its charity, its example and prayer, collaborates in their conversion'. The Council allowed for the continuation of the secret confessional, a practice introduced in the seventeenth century, but also sanctioned face-to-face conversations outside the confessional between the priest and the person seeking absolution. Although this allows the priest to know the identity of the penitent he is still bound by the confidentiality of the 'seal of confession'.

The Sacrament of Reconciliation requires that those who repent of their sins should:
- **be contrite.** Contrition includes both a genuine sorrow for one's sins and a determination not to commit them again. 'Perfect' contrition comes from the love of God forgiving all kinds of sins. 'Imperfect' contrition also comes from God but stems from the fear of eternal damnation and hell. Both are acceptable.
- **confess their sins.** An examination of one's conscience in the light of the Ten Commandments and the Sermon on the Mount is very important. Confession is not only good for the soul but it also encourages us to take responsibility for our sinful actions. Saying our sins out loud to the priest, God's representative, shows that we have owned up and accepted responsibility for them.
- **seek absolution.** Absolution means 'to clear from guilt or blame'. The authority to forgive sins given originally by Jesus to his apostles (see Extract 1) became the responsibility of the Church after their deaths. Through it, bishops and priests are able to claim God's forgiveness for the sinner.

The sacrament of reconciliation

After greeting and blessing the penitent the confessor reads a short passage from the Bible. Next, the penitent confesses his or her sins and offers an act of contrition. The priest gives a suitable penance before saying the words of absolution. The short liturgy concludes with a prayer of praise and thanksgiving followed by the dismissal and blessing by the priest.

Confessions to the priest, whether in secret or face to face, are a common fact of parish life. Most churches hold confessions each Saturday and whenever required. During certain liturgical seasons, however, such as Lent, many parishes have communal celebrations of the Sacrament of Reconciliation. These special services include readings from the Scriptures, a common examination of the conscience, a homily from the priest, the Lord's Prayer and hymns. These communal celebrations of the sacrament also include the opportunity for personal confession and so they may involve many priests. A common prayer of confession by those assembled may lead to a general absolution being given to the whole congregation.

The sacrament of reconciliation is a very important part of the spiritual journey for most Catholics. It is the way that has been set aside for reaching reconciliation with God and with his Church. It is also the way that God has set aside to offer personal forgiveness to sinners.

WORK TO DO

1 Describe the Sacrament of Reconciliation.

2 Explain what part the sacrament of reconciliation might play in the life of a Roman Catholic.

3 Read Extract 3 from the CCC carefully. Rewrite it in your own words to show that you understand what it means.

4 During the Sacrament of Reconciliation the priest says: 'May God give you pardon and peace . . . I absolve you from your sins.' What has the penitent had to show before the priest can grant an absolution?

5 If forgiving others is the responsibility of every Christian why do you think there is a need for the Sacrament of Reconciliation?

What part does the Sacrament of Reconciliation play in the spiritual life of a Roman Catholic?

DISCUSSION POINT

When a priest hears a person's confession do you think he is simply acting as a counsellor, or is there more involvement than that?

What role does the priest play in the confessional?

KEY WORDS

Absolution
Apostle
Baptism
Bishop
Confirmation
Eucharist
Holy Spirit
Homily
Lent
Liturgy
Lord's Prayer
Penance
Priest
Sermon on the Mount
Ten commandments

8 SEX AND MARRIAGE

8.1 SEX OUTSIDE MARRIAGE

The Roman Catholic Church teaches that all forms of sexual activity outside marriage are wrong. This includes adultery, fornication and homosexual intercourse. The ccc underlines the traditional teaching of the Church on sexual morality, arguing strongly in favour of chastity.

KEY QUESTION

What does the Roman Catholic Church teach about chastity, fornication and adultery?

CONSULT

Matthew 5:27–30

Extract 1

There are three forms of the virtue of chastity: the first is that of spouses, the second that of widows and the third that of virgins. We do not praise any of them to the exclusion of the others ... This is what makes for the richness of discipline of the Church.

St Ambrose, an early Christian bishop

Extract 2

Fornication is carnal union between an unmarried man and an unmarried woman. It is gravely contrary to the dignity of persons and of human sexuality which is naturally ordered to the good of spouses ...

CCC (2353)

Chastity

Chastity, abstaining from sexual activity and intercourse, can take various forms, as Extract 1 shows. It includes:

- **chastity in marriage** This involves two people being completely faithful to each other – what the CCC calls 'conjugal chastity'. This faithfulness should be the norm for every Catholic marriage.
- **chastity for widows** For those who have lost a partner chastity means abstaining from sexual activity unless they remarry. Looking after the welfare of widows was a top priority in early Christian communities.
- **chastity for virgins** A virgin is someone who has not had any sexual experience. A virgin is expected to remain chaste until he or she marries. Those engaged should consider their time of engagement as an opportunity to discover: '... a mutual respect, an apprenticeship in fidelity and the hope of receiving one another from God' (CCC 2350).

Chastity does not come easily to human beings. Human sexual feelings are very strong and, when aroused, almost overwhelming. This is why a deliberate attempt needs to be made to control them or else they will control us. These feelings are most difficult to control during adolescence when they are at their strongest. By controlling them a Catholic is being faithful to his or her baptismal vows.

Sex outside marriage

Fornication covers any heterosexual intercourse between people who are not married to each other. From the teachings of Jesus and the New Testament writings of Paul onwards, fornication has always been considered to be a serious moral evil. This is because the only proper place for sexual intercourse is within marriage. There are various reasons for this:

1 The teaching from Genesis, emphasised by Jesus, is of two people 'becoming one flesh' i.e., united in sexual intercourse, in marriage. Such unity cannot apply outside marriage.

2 Sex outside marriage risks creating children. Minimising the risk by using artificial contraception is unacceptable for a Roman Catholic (see 8.4 and 8.5).

3 Sex outside marriage cheapens, and trivialises, an act which is one of God's greatest gifts to the human race. God has decreed that sexual intercourse be confined to marriage because that is the only relationship in which it has its true meaning.

4 It excludes the sacrament which was intended by Christ to protect and make marriage, and sexual intercourse, holy.

Adultery

Adultery is sexual intercourse between a married person and someone who is not his or her spouse. Under the law given to the Jews by Moses, adultery was punishable by death by stoning. Jesus adopted a much more humane and understanding attitude when he was confronted by a woman accused of adultery (John 8:1–11) but he still condemned the practice (Mark 10:19). The Roman Catholic Church teaches that adultery is contrary to the sixth commandment ('You shall not commit adultery') and breaks the trust which must exist between a husband and wife in a marriage which is blessed by God.

WORK TO DO

1 Explain the meaning of each of the following:
   a) celibacy
   b) chastity
   c) virginity
   d) extra-marital sex
   e) adultery
   f) promiscuity.

2 Why might a Christian regard adultery as wrong?

3 Explain why the Catholic Church is opposed to sex before marriage.

4 On what basis does the Church argue that marriage is still the only proper place for sexual activity to take place?

Extract 3

> You have heard that it was said, 'Do not commit adultery'. But I tell you that anyone who looks at a woman lustfully has already committed adultery with her in his heart.

Matthew 5:27,28

What does the Roman Catholic Church require of this couple before they marry?

DISCUSSION POINT

What do you think is involved in living a chaste life in the twenty-first century?

KEY WORDS

Adultery
Chastity
Fornication
Heterosexuality
Homosexuality
New Testament
Paul
Sacrament
Second World War

8.2 MARRIAGE

KEY QUESTION

What are the most important elements in a Christian marriage and how are these reflected in the wedding service?

CONSULT

Mark 10:6–8

Extract 1

How shall we be ever able to adequately describe the happiness of that marriage which the Church arranges, which the sacrifice strengthens, upon which the blessing sets a seal, at which the angels are present as witnesses, and to which the Father gives his consent?

Tertullian, third-century Church leader

Extract 2

I call upon these persons here present to witness that I do take thee to be my lawful wedded husband/wife; to have and to hold from this day forward; for better, for worse, for richer, for poorer, in sickness and in health; to love and to cherish; till death us do part.

The marriage vows

In the Catholic Church marriage is a sacrament. In this sacrament a baptised man and woman give their love to each other in an exclusive, permanent, sexual relationship. Their union with each other is marked, and distinguished, by love, care and respect. They are committed to share responsibility for the bringing up of children if God should so bless them.

Marriage in the Bible

In the story of creation in Genesis, God gives to 'man' the task of naming all the animals (Genesis 2:19,20). He does so but is unable to find a 'helpmate' (soulmate) among them and so God makes 'woman' from one of his ribs. Man is delighted with his new soulmate: 'This at last is bone of my bones and flesh from my flesh! This is to be called woman for this was taken from man' (Genesis 2:23). The writer then added: 'This is why a man leaves his father and mother and joins himself to his wife, and they become one body' (Genesis 2:24).

The implication of this is clear. When they marry, a man and a woman leave their home, and parents, and set up a new home of their own. The sexual union between them is basic to their new relationship – they become 'one flesh'. The new relationship was then given a clear task by God: 'Be fruitful, multiply, fill the earth and conquer it' (Genesis 1:28). The Roman Catholic Church accepts that the procreation of children is a basic, God-given reason for marriage. Jesus blessed marriage by performing his first miracle at the wedding feast in Cana of Galilee (John 2:1–11). He underlined his belief in the importance of marriage by taking a strong stand against divorce (Matthew 19:3–12).

The sacrament of matrimony

In the sacrament of matrimony, the Nuptial Mass, the couple minister the sacrament to each other. This makes matrimony unique amongst the sacraments since in the others the bishop, or the priest, is the agent of God's blessing. The Sacrament of Marriage in a Catholic church usually takes place during a celebration of the Mass. By celebrating in this way the couple are placing their love for each other within the sacrificial love that Christ has for them and the Church. The Sacrament of Reconciliation beforehand also provides the couple with the opportunity to confess any sins before they are married.

The wedding liturgy includes prayers, readings, hymns and a homily. After these the priest questions the couple on their freedom to marry, their commitment to being faithful and their willingness to have, and bring up, children. The bridal couple then exchange their vows (see Extract 2). The husband and wife exchange rings, saying: 'Take this ring as a sign of my love and fidelity. In the name of the Father, and of the Son and of the Holy Spirit.'

The priest draws the wedding ceremony to a close. After prayers for the couple and the signing of the register, the service moves into the Mass. During the Mass the priest prays that the couple will:

- always stay true to God's commandments
- be kept faithful in marriage
- be living examples of the Christian life.

Finally, after communion, the priest reminds the couple that they must be faithful witnesses to the love of God in a needy world.

WORK TO DO

1 a) State two promises made during a Christian wedding service.
   b) Why are these promises important to Christian people?
   c) How can a couple show that they are committed to each other?

2 What meaning is attached to the wedding ring given, and often exchanged, in the wedding service?

3 What vows do the bride and groom make to each other during the wedding service and what do they mean?

4 Describe three pieces of symbolism found in the Catholic wedding service.

5 a) Why is a church wedding such an important start to married life for Christian couples?
   b) What does a church wedding stress about marriage?

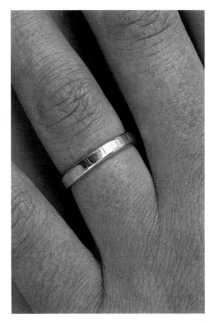

Why is a ring a perfect symbol of the love between a man and a woman?

DISCUSSION POINT

What does it mean when the Catholic Church describes marriage as a sacrament?

This couple have been married for a long time. What do you think is the main secret of a happy and successful marriage?

Extract 3

May you always bear witness to the love of God in this world so that the afflicted and the needy will find in you generous friends, and welcome you into the joys of heaven.

Concluding prayer in the marriage ceremony

KEY QUESTION

What is the distinctive teaching of the Roman Catholic Church about family life?

CONSULT

Colossians 3:18–21

Extract 1

I have been reminded of your sincere faith, which first lived in your grandmother Lois and in your mother Eunice and, I am persuaded, now lives in you also.

2 Timothy 1:5

The health of the family unit and the health of the Church are inextricably bound up with each other. The Second Vatican Council referred to the Catholic family as the 'domestic church'. It went on to say: 'The Christian family . . . will show forth to all . . . the authentic nature of the Church.' This phrase also found favour with Popes Paul VI, John Paul I and John Paul II. The term suggests that the community of faith, the Church, begins in the home, in the family unit. It is the family which begets new members of the Church. It is in the family that faith in God is transmitted by word and example, both within and beyond the home. To quote Pope Paul VI: 'There should be found in every Christian family the various aspects of the entire Church.' During a visit to the USA in 1987 Pope John Paul II reminded everyone that family life is central to parish life. Every parish is a family of families. The spiritual vitality of a parish depends on the spiritual life to be found in its families.

Family life

Catholic couples are expected to make their family life the first priority of their married lives together. Couples know from their own early experience that they need to base their family life on trust, forgiveness and commitment. They know, too, that they need to take seriously their commitment to each other until death separates them, since divorce has a devastating effect on all family members. Faced by the pressures of modern life they know the importance of prayer and the Mass in keeping married life stable and fulfilling. Today the Church seeks to support them in maintaining a strong family life through different retreat programmes which are designed to strengthen and enrich married life.

The CCC calls the family 'the original cell of social life'. It goes on to insist that family life is the place where children learn:
- moral values, the difference between right and wrong
- to honour God
- to make good use of the freedom they are increasingly given.

What can this family provide for its youngest member to allow him to grow into a healthy adult?

How is the love of a mother for her baby like the love of the Church for each of its members?

Responsibilities and duties

The New Testament reminds believers of the duties and responsibilities that parents and children within a family have to each other. The CCC underlines:

- **the duties of children**   Respect for parents (filial piety) comes from the gratitude felt by children for those who have given them the gifts of life and love which have enabled them to grow in wisdom and grace. In return they are expected to show 'true docility and obedience' to their parents. Catholics should be particularly thankful to those who have handed their faith down to them and encouraged it to grow. This extends beyond parents to grandparents, other members of the family, pastors, catechists and other teachers and friends.
- **the responsibilities of parents**   The responsibilities of parents towards young children are total and all-embracing – physical, social, moral and spiritual. Parents are the 'first heralds of faith' to their children. The CCC tells them that: 'They should associate them [their children] from their tenderest years with the life of the Church.' They are responsible for creating a home in which tenderness, forgiveness, respect and service are the rule. They must set a good example to their children in all ways.

Finally, the Church also remembers those couples who are childless and people who remain single. Those who cannot have children for whatever reason (about 10 per cent of all couples) can still enjoy a married life that is full of love and meaning. Those who have given themselves to the single life should always be able to find a real family of love and support in the Catholic Church community.

WORK TO DO

1 The Roman Catholic Church speaks of the family as being the 'domestic church'.
   a) What does it mean by this phrase?
   b) How important is family life to the health of the Roman Catholic Church?

2 Why do most people, and the Roman Catholic Church, think that family life is important?

3 a) What do you think are the most important features of family life?
   b) What would you miss most if family life was abolished?

4 Outline the teaching of the Roman Catholic Church about the importance of family life.

5 'A Catholic family needs to worship together to stay together.' Do you agree?

6 Write down three ways in which the Church helps in the bringing up and spiritual growth of children.

Extract 2

Children, obey your parents in everything, for this pleases the Lord. Fathers, do not embitter your children, or they will become discouraged.

Colossians 3:18–21

Extract 3

The family was ordained of God . . . It was before the Church, or rather the first form of the Church on earth.

Pope Leo XIII, 1880

DISCUSSION POINT

What do you think it means in practice for married couples to put their family at the centre of their lives?

KEY WORDS

Mass
New Testament
Second Vatican Council

CONTRACEPTION – THE FACTS

Contraception (contra-conception), or birth control, is the attempt to prevent conception taking place after sexual intercourse. The Roman Catholic Church teaches that contraception by artificial means is always wrong but it does encourage the use of natural methods of birth control. You will discover the reasons for this teaching in 8.5.

KEY QUESTION

What are the main natural and artificial forms of contraception?

Church teaching

The Catholic opposition to contraception, going back to the early centuries of the Church, was supported later by the Orthodox Church in the East and by Protestants in the West. Pope Leo XIII, in a major encyclical on marriage published in 1880, did not even mention contraception. The first Lambeth Conference of the Anglican Church held after the First World War taught that the use of contraception was morally and spiritually indefensible. By the next Conference, held in 1930, however, the Church and its leaders had changed its collective mind. Soon other Protestant Churches, such as the Methodists, came out strongly in support of the responsible use of contraception in a married relationship. The Eastern Orthodox Church also expressed its support for contraception within marriage as a means of bringing about responsible parenthood.

During his short papacy Pope John XXIII (1958–63) set up a commission to look at the whole issue of birth control and family planning. After Pope Paul VI had succeeded Pope John, the commission presented two reports reflecting the differences of opinion among its members. The majority report recommended a change in the Church's attitude to contraception whilst the minority report urged the Pope to hold fast to traditional teaching. Pope Paul VI supported the minority view and published, in 1968, his encyclical *Humanae Vitae* (*On the regulation of birth*). Condemning artificial contraception, such as the Pill and the condom, the Pope insisted that: '. . . every marriage act must remain open to the transmission of life'. This remains the teaching of the Roman Catholic Church today.

Extract 1

> God blessed them and said to them, 'Be fruitful and increase in number; fill the earth and subdue it.'

Genesis 1:28

Unnatural and natural family planning

Amongst the artificial methods of contraception condemned by the Roman Catholic Church are:

- **the Pill**   Over 3 million women in the UK and 50 million worldwide use this method. It claims to offer almost 100 per cent reliability, although some women experience side effects from taking it.
- **the IUD or coil**   Inserted into a woman's uterus by a doctor and left in place, the IUD brings about a 'spontaneous abortion' (miscarriage) if a fertilised egg embeds itself in the wall of the uterus. This makes it an 'abortifacient', i.e., a device designed to secure an abortion.
- **the cap or diaphragm**   This is a circular rubber device which a woman fits over the neck of her cervix before sex, so preventing the sperm from reaching the fallopian tubes and uterus.
- **the condom or sheath**   This is a tube of thin latex which a man fits over his erect penis before he has any sexual contact

Extract 2

> Sons are a heritage from the Lord, children a reward from him. Like arrows in the hands of a warrior are sons born in one's youth. Blessed is the man whose quiver is full of them.

Psalm 127:4,5

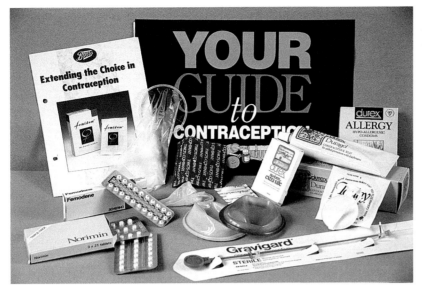

On what is the Roman Catholic objection to most forms of birth control based?

with his partner. Apart from being a contraceptive the condom offers protection against sexually transmitted diseases including HIV.

- **sterilisation** In the man's case the tube which carries the sperm from the testicles to the penis is cut and in a woman's case the fallopian tubes are cauterised. This is particularly unacceptable to the Roman Catholic Church as it makes the man or the woman infertile and so rules out the possibility of any further pregnancy.

Natural family planning involves monitoring a woman's menstrual cycle to determine whether she is fertile or infertile. This is acceptable to the Roman Catholic Church because it does not involve any interruption to the act of sexual intercourse or the natural process of conception. The form of the 'rhythm' method which was often used in the past was based upon a calendar calculation of the woman's most fertile period. This was not very reliable. The modern form, also called the symptothermal method, involves taking a woman's body temperature as soon as she wakes up, and checking the shape and position of the cervix and the quantity and consistency of the vaginal mucus. This information gives a more reliable guide to her fertility.

WORK TO DO

1 In 1984 the Pope said: 'Only natural forms of birth control do not offend moral law established by God.'
   a) What are natural forms of birth control?
   b) Name three 'unnatural' forms of birth control.
   c) How might unnatural forms of birth control offend 'the moral order established by God'?

2 What is an artificial means of birth control?

3 Describe the forms of birth control that a Roman Catholic is free to use.

Extract 3

. . . condemned is any action, which either before, or at the moment of, or after sexual intercourse is specifically intended to prevent procreation – whether it is an ends or a means . . . It is never lawful, even for the gravest reasons, to do evil, that good may come of it.

Humanae Vitae, 1968

DISCUSSION POINT

What is your attitude to contraception?

KEY WORDS

Anglican Church
Methodist Church
Natural family planning
Orthodox Church
Protestant

The Catholic Church teaches that sex has been given by God to married couples both for their enjoyment and for the continuation of the human race. Both of these ends are in the nature of the gift itself and so must be present whenever sexual intercourse takes place. If they are not present then God's good gift is being misused. It follows, then, that every sexual act must be open to the possibility of creating new life at all times.

In *Casti Canubii*, published in 1930, Pope Pius IX expressed the opposition of the Church to all artificial forms of birth control for this reason. In 1951 Pope Pius XII allowed Catholics to use the rhythm method (restricting sexual intercourse to a woman's infertile period) as this worked in harmony with the body's natural pattern. Then, in 1968, *Humanae Vitae* insisted that the rhythm method was the only acceptable form of contraception for Catholics to use. This, though, has not ended the debate. No aspect of moral behaviour causes more heated debate among Roman Catholics than that of contraception.

Do you agree with the teaching of the Catholic Church that the natural function of the sexual act is always to conceive a child?

Why people use contraception

Many Christians, including some Roman Catholics, would argue for the responsible use of contraception on the following grounds:

- Whilst reproduction is one of the basic reasons for sex it is not necessarily the most important at all times. God has also given sex in marriage so that a couple can enjoy their love for each other and express that love openly.
- Modern contraception gives married couples an element of choice not enjoyed by previous generations. Couples today do not need to run the risk of pregnancy unless they have made a conscious decision to start or extend their family.
- Contraception allows women to enjoy better health and a career of their own if they choose. The overall standard of living, and the educational opportunities, for the children already in the family are raised. At the same time, a couple are not prevented from having a large family if they wish.
- Properly used contraception removes the fear of an unwanted pregnancy and provides the man and the woman with a sense of security in their love-making. Fear is one of the major causes of impotence in many men.

Arguments against contraception

In 1981 the document *The Christian Family in the Modern World* warned Catholics about the dangers of adopting a 'contraceptive mentality'. This mentality looks upon contraception as a solution to all kinds of personal problems. The strong antipathy of the Church towards contraception has been maintained on the following grounds:

- Contraception has always been condemned by the Church and this condemnation forms one of the most important planks in its moral teaching. The Church has always insisted that deliberately interfering with the sexual act to prevent conception is a grave moral sin. Such a strong tradition cannot be set aside.

- Contraception is wrong because it interferes with the natural function of the sexual act, which is to conceive a child. The sexual act must always remain open to this possibility. That is the main purpose given by God to sex since the creation.
- Many artificial means of birth control use methods which are morally indefensible. The IUD or coil, for instance, works by causing the already joined sperm and egg to be flushed out of the woman's body, so bringing about an early abortion. This is always a grave sin.
- Natural family planning, or 'periodic continence' as the CCC calls it, has been much improved in recent years and can now offer a reliable alternative for those Roman Catholics who have strong reasons for wishing to delay a pregnancy. Most importantly, it does not ask a Roman Catholic to act in a way that is contrary to their religious faith.

WORK TO DO

1 What do you understand the Roman Catholic Church to mean when it says that every act of sexual intercourse should be open to the possibility of new life?

2 Why has the teaching of the Roman Catholic Church on contraception caused such controversy?

3 Give three reasons why the Roman Catholic Church is opposed to all methods of artificial birth control.

4 a) Describe two opposing Christian points of view about contraception.
   b) State which of them you agree with and explain why.

Extract 1

A particular aspect of responsibility concerns the regulation of births. For just reasons, spouses may wish to space the births of their children. It is their duty to make certain that their desire is not motivated by selfishness but is in conformity with the generosity appropriate to responsible parenthood.

CCC (2368)

Extract 2

Every action which, whether in anticipation of the conjugal [sexual] act, or in its accomplishment . . . proposes, whether as an act or a means, to render procreation impossible is intrinsically evil.

Humanae Vitae, 1968

8.6 MARITAL BREAKDOWN (1)

KEY QUESTION

Why are there so many divorces in the United Kingdom?

Extract 1

> To the married I give this command (not I, but the Lord): A wife must not separate from her husband. But if she does, she must remain unmarried or be reconciled to her husband. And a husband must not divorce his wife.

1 Corinthians 7:10,11

Extract 2

> Divorce is a grave offence against the natural law. It claims to break the contract, to which the spouses freely consent, to live with each other till death. Divorce does injury to the covenant of salvation, of which sacramental marriage is the sign. Contracting a new union, even if it is recognised by civil law, adds to the gravity of the rupture . . .

CCC (2384)

The rate of marital breakdown, including divorce, is steadily rising in every Western society. Marital breakdown can be divided into three separate categories:

- **divorce.** This is the legal termination of a marriage. We know how many divorces take place in each country year by year since a divorce can only be granted by a court of law.
- **separation.** This means that the husband and wife no longer live together but they have not divorced (although that may follow later). They may be separated legally or have an informal arrangement with each other. Either way, there is no way of telling how many married couples are living separate lives.
- **'empty-shell' marriages.** This is when a couple live together and remain legally married but their marriage exists in name only. The number of people living in empty-shell marriages is unknowable.

Divorce in the UK

Before 1857 divorce was a long-drawn-out and very costly affair, with the result that only a handful of couples went through the process each year. The Matrimonial Causes Act of 1857 simplified the divorce procedure and made it possible, for the first time, for both men and women to begin divorce proceedings. However, it remained much easier for a man to divorce his wife than vice versa round for two reasons:

- a woman had to demonstrate that her husband had committed adultery and another 'matrimonial offence', such as desertion or cruelty.
- a man only had to prove that his wife had been unfaithful.

In 1923 men and women were given the same legal rights to divorce. Fourteen years later the grounds for divorce were extended beyond adultery to include desertion, cruelty and insanity. Both partners, though, had to agree to the divorce. In 1968, the Divorce Reform Act changed the emphasis of the law by allowing people to divorce if they could demonstrate that their marriage had 'irretrievably broken down'. Adultery, cruelty and desertion could be used to demonstrate this. A couple could divorce if only one partner wanted it, but only after a five-year separation. If both partners agreed then a divorce could be granted after two years of separation. In both cases, though, the judge had to be sure that satisfactory arrangements had been made for any children involved.

The aftermath

This legislation changed the divorce situation radically. The number of people seeking a divorce rose rapidly and now stands at around 180,000 a year. Over the same period the number of people marrying for the first time has declined until today, at below 200,000 a year, it barely exceeds those seeking a divorce. Amongst the consequences of the sharp increase in the divorce rate we may list the following:

- there are now more than 1.2 million single-parent families in the UK. The vast majority of these have been created by divorce. It is thought that more than one in three of all children born since 1971 have found themselves living in families affected by divorce or separation. Seventy-five per cent of all divorcing couples have children under the age of 16.

- many couples no longer see marriage as a life-long commitment. Instead of working hard at their marriage when problems arise, they take the easy way out.
- easy divorce devalues marriage at a time when the relationship is more important than ever. The proportion of unmarried men and women over the age of 18 who are cohabiting (living with a partner but not married to them) is now 25 per cent – compared with just over 10 per cent in 1981.

WORK TO DO

1 Define each of the following:
   a) divorce
   b) separation
   c) 'empty-shell' marriages.

2 a) What happened in 1857 to make divorce easier?
   b) How was the law changed in 1923?
   c) What changes were made to the divorce law in 1968?

3 List three consequences of making divorce easier to obtain in the United Kingdom.

What do you think can be done to protect children from the bad effects of a divorce?

What particular problems do you think one-parent families, like this one, face?

8.7 MARITAL BREAKDOWN (2)

KEY QUESTION

Why is the Roman Catholic Church opposed to divorce?

CONSULT

Matthew 5:31,32
and 19:3–9;
Mark 10:9; 1
Corinthians 7:10,11

The CCC refers to two main offences which people can commit against the dignity of marriage:

1 Adultery   When two people, one of whom is already married to someone else, have sexual relations, then adultery has been committed. The sixth commandment ('Thou shalt not commit adultery') and the New Testament generally condemn adultery. The Old Testament prophets denounced adultery as 'an image of the sin of idolatry' (see Hosea 2:7). Jesus condemned not only adultery but also adulterous thoughts (Matthew 5:27,28).

2 Divorce   The Roman Catholic Church finds the legal termination of a marriage (divorce) impossible for the following reasons:

- Jesus insisted that it was the original intention of the Creator God that marriage should be indissoluble (Matthew 5:31–32). He even rejected the somewhat lax attitude to divorce that had crept into the Jewish faith (Matthew 19:7–9).
- divorce is a grave offence against natural law. It claims to be able to break the marriage contract in which two people freely agreed to live together until death parted them. Entering into a new marriage commitment after divorce is the same as committing adultery. Jesus said as much (see Matthew 5:31,32).
- divorce is immoral because it brings disorder into a family. Many people suffer greatly as a result – especially the deserted husband or wife, and children who are often traumatised by the separation of their parents and torn emotionally between them. The CCC draws a sharp distinction between someone who is innocently affected by divorce and 'one who through his own grave fault destroys a canonically valid marriage'.

Extract 1

Between the baptised a ratified and consummated marriage cannot be dissolved by any human power or for any reason other than death.

Codex Iuris Canonici, 1983

Annulment and separation

The commonest way for a Roman Catholic to end a marriage is to obtain an annulment from a Church tribunal, which carries out a full investigation. Since the granting of annulments was transferred from the Vatican to local tribunals the number granted each year has increased considerably. In granting an annulment the Church does not deny that a loving relationship may once have existed but simply states that the marriage was never valid in the eyes of the Church. There are a total of 12 reasons for granting an annulment, including:

- one of the partners not having given their free and full consent to the marriage. The CCC underlines that such consent must be 'free of coercion and grave external fear' (CCC, 1628).
- one spouse not understanding the full implications of the marriage relationship when they married.
- the marriage not having been consummated, i.e., sexual intercourse has not taken place.

The Roman Catholic Church does allow separation. This may be a very painful, but necessary, answer to the problems that a couple are suffering.

Consequences in the Church

Divorce leaves people feeling very bruised and vulnerable. The Church has a responsibility to maintain its discipline but, at the same time, to care for those affected by divorce. Those who have divorced and remarried without Church approval cannot receive the sacraments, especially Holy Communion. In the past people in such a situation may have been excommunicated but this practice has now ceased. Pope John Paul II has underlined more than once the responsibility of the Church to react in a loving and understanding way to those suffering from the trauma of divorce. At the same time Church leaders are concerned to improve marriage preparation and support for those who are married, to cut down on the number of failed and broken relationships.

WORK TO DO

1 The Roman Catholic Church teaches that divorce is wrong. What reasons does it give for this teaching?

2 What help does the Roman Catholic Church offer to couples who have problems in their married lives? You will need to carry out research of your own to answer this question.

3 What is adultery and why is it condemned unreservedly by the Roman Catholic Church?

4 'Until death us do part.' How do Roman Catholics understand this part of the marriage service?

What is the difference between a divorce and an annulment?

Extract 2

There is a considerable difference between a spouse who has sincerely tried to be faithful to the sacrament of marriage and is unjustly abandoned, and one who through his own grave fault destroys a canonically valid marriage.

CCC (2386)

DISCUSSION POINT

Do you share the view of the Roman Catholic Church that marriage is an unbreakable bond between two people, made in the presence of God? If so, why?

KEY WORDS

Adultery
Annulment
Divorce
Holy Communion
New Testament
Old Testament
Sacrament

CONSULT

Leviticus 18:22; 1 Corinthians 6:9,10

Extract 1

Tradition has always declared that 'homosexual acts are intrinsically disordered'. They are contrary to natural law. They close the sexual act to the gift of life . . . Under no circumstances can they be approved.

CCC (2357)

Although no one can be sure, it is thought that about 10 per cent of the population (6 per cent of men and 4 per cent of women) are homosexual. Still more are 'bisexual', i.e., they are sexually attracted to both men and women.

Three terms are used to describe people who prefer same-sex relationships:

- **Homosexual** Homosexuality (from the Latin *homo* meaning 'same') applies to sexual relationships between members of the same sex, male and female. Although homosexual activity has taken place since early times – it was well known by the time of the ancient Greeks, for example – it was not until 1869 that the word itself was coined, by Karoly Benkert, a Hungarian doctor. By giving such relationships a name he was emphasising that homosexuals were not frustrated heterosexuals but a distinct group with their own sexual interests and motivations.
- **Lesbian** This word was first used in the nineteenth century to describe female homosexuals and was taken from the name of the island of Lesbos where, in the seventh century BCE, the female Greek poet Sappho gathered an all-female community around herself.
- **Gay** In recent years most male homosexuals have preferred to be called 'gay'. This term, first adopted in the 1970s, was a conscious attempt to counteract the popular idea that homosexuals were miserable people with a secret longing to be heterosexual.

The term 'homophobia' was coined in 1967 to describe the irrational fear that some people have about homosexuality. This stems from the many negative beliefs that some people have about the homosexual lifestyle, which are similar to those associated with other prejudices, such as racism.

Homosexuality and the law

Until 1967 it was illegal for any man in England and Wales to be a practising homosexual (there has never been a law against lesbianism). Many gay men were prosecuted; others were vulnerable to blackmail from people threatening to expose their sexual activities to their families or the public. Since 1967 homosexual relationships have been permitted as long as they are:

- conducted between consenting adults aged 21 and over. In 1994 this age limit was reduced to 18. An attempt to bring it into line with laws covering heterosexual activity, making homosexual sex lawful at the age of 16, was initially defeated but later passed.
- carried out in private.

The Roman Catholic Church and homosexuality

It is generally agreed today that homosexuality is a natural sexual orientation, not a lifestyle choice. It is only comparatively recently, however, that a line has been drawn between the homosexual orientation (tendency) and homosexual activity. Two consequences have followed from this:

- All of the major Christian Churches, including the Roman Catholic Church, refuse to condemn the sexual orientation which draws a person physically to members of their own sex rather than the opposite sex. A homosexual is given the same dignity in the sight of God as a heterosexual.
- Homosexual activity remains immoral. It cannot meet the criteria laid down by the Catholic Church for all acceptable sexual activity, which are that it must be confined to marriage, leaving itself open to the transmission of new life and so on. Catholic teaching about human sexuality has always been grounded in the description in Genesis of the man and the woman becoming 'one flesh' and this means that heterosexual genital expression is the norm. At the same time the Catholic Church has tried to treat individual homosexuals non-judgementally and with great sensitivity.

WORK TO DO

1 a) What is homosexuality?
   b) Why do you think that the CCC says that 'under no circumstances can [homosexual acts] be approved'?
   c) Do you agree with this teaching? Explain your answer.

2 Explain the meaning of these terms:
   a) homosexual
   b) gay
   c) lesbian.

3 Read carefully the three extracts from the CCC. Write two paragraphs summing up what the Catechism teaches about homosexuality and how it should be dealt with in the local church.

4 Imagine that you are a Roman Catholic priest. You have a homosexual couple as regular members of your congregation. Bearing in mind the teaching of the Catechism, how would you treat them?

Would you agree that society finds it easier to accept sexual relations between women than between men?

Extract 2

> [Homosexuals] must be accepted with respect, compassion and sensitivity. Every sign of unjust discrimination in their regard should be avoided. These persons are called to fulfil God's will in their lives and, if they are Christians, to unite to the sacrifice of the Lord's Cross the difficulties they may encounter from their condition.

CCC (2358)

Extract 3

> Homosexual persons are called to chastity. By the virtues of self-mastery that teach them inner freedom, at times by the support of disinterested friendship, by prayer and sacramental grace, they can and should gradually and resolutely approach Christian perfection.

CCC (2359)

DISCUSSION POINT

Are you happy with the view of most Churches that homosexual orientation is acceptable but that homosexual behaviour is not?

KEY WORDS
Heterosexuality
Homosexuality
Lesbian

9 MATTERS OF LIFE AND DEATH

9.1 ANOINTING THE SICK

Anointing the sick is one of the seven sacraments celebrated by the Roman Catholic Church. For centuries this sacrament, called 'extreme unction' (the last anointing), was linked with dying. In 1972, though, Pope Paul VI linked it with the strengthening of the faith of those who are ill or old. This new emphasis is at the heart of the sacrament and its place in the life of the Church today.

The Sacrament of the Sick

In the Gospels Jesus healed many people (see, for example, Matthew 8:2–4; Mark 1:30–31; Luke 5:18–25; Mark 3:1–5 and Matthew 17:14–18) as well as sending out his disciples to continue his healing work. Mark tells us that they cast out many demons, anointed sick people with oil and healed them. After Jesus left the earth, healing was an important part of the ministry of the apostles (see Acts 3:1–10 and 5:12–16 for examples of this).

By offering the Sacrament of the Sick to those in need the Church is following in the footsteps of Jesus and his apostles. The sacrament reassures the sick that God is with them and that the Church is praying for them (see Extract 3). Its celebration falls into three parts:

1 Friends and relatives are invited to share in the service along with the sick person. The priest sprinkles them with holy water saying: 'Let this water call to mind our baptism in Christ, who by his death and resurrection has redeemed us.' The people confess their sins and receive absolution. The priest reminds everyone of the words of James (see 9.2) before laying hands on the person. This common Roman Catholic practice goes back to the Old Testament and symbolises:
- the giving of strength in a time of great need
- the gift of the Holy Spirit
- the touch of healing.

2 The priest anoints the person's forehead with oil, saying: 'through this holy anointing may the Lord in his love and mercy help you with the grace of the Holy Spirit' and then he anoints their hands as well.

3 Mass is celebrated. If the person taking Mass is dying then the bread and wine provide the *viaticum* (food for the journey). After exchanging the sign of peace with the priest and everyone present the person is reminded of their baptismal vows and encouraged to trust in God for this, their final journey.

KEY QUESTION

What is the Sacrament of the Sick and what part does it play in the life of the Roman Catholic Church today?

CONSULT

Mark 6:12,13

Extract 1

When it was evening, they brought to him all who were ill or possessed by demons. The whole town was gathered at the door. He cured many who were sick with various diseases, and he drove out many demons . . .

Mark 1:32–34

Extract 2

Heal the sick! The Church has received this charge from the Lord and strives to carry it out by taking care of the sick as well as by accompanying them with her prayer of intercession.

CCC (1509)

The symbols

Three important symbolic acts take place in this sacrament:

1 Sprinkling with holy water. This is a reminder that, through baptism, the sick person was called to follow Christ and to share in his work. Now, through suffering, they are sharing in his death.

2 The laying on of hands. As with the early Christians this act symbolises the giving of God's Holy Spirit. He alone can give the power to come to terms with illness, suffering and death.

3 Anointing the head and hands. This practice was followed by Jesus and his disciples, although its roots are found in the earlier Jewish community. Then, as now, the oil symbolised healing, comfort and God's blessing.

WORK TO DO

1 Describe one occasion on which Jesus anointed the sick.

2 a) What is the Sacrament of the Sick?
   b) How does a priest administer the sacrament?
   c) Why do you think this sacrament is important for those who are ill or old?

3 What is the viaticum?

4 Explain the symbolic importance of the following in the sacrament of anointing the sick:
   a) sprinkling with holy water
   b) laying on of hands
   c) anointing with oil.

5 Why do you think it is important for the Church to continue the healing work begun by Jesus and his disciples?

6 a) Put the words of John Paul II in Extract 4 into your own words.
   b) What do you think the Pope meant when he described the poor, the sick and the elderly as demonstrating that 'weakness is a creative part of human living'?

Extract 3

Do not neglect your sick and elderly. Do not turn away from the handicapped and the dying. Do not push them to the margins of society. For if you do, you will fail to understand that they represent an important truth . . . that weakness is a creative part of human living.

Pope John Paul II

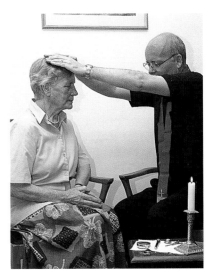

Why does the priest lay his hands on the head of the sick person?

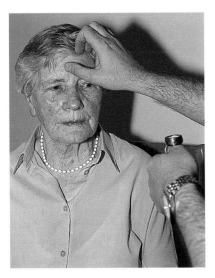

What does the oil in the Sacrament of the Sick symbolise?

DISCUSSION POINT

Why do you think that many Catholics find the Sacrament of the Sick very comforting?

KEY WORDS

Absolution
Apostle
Baptism
Disciple
Extreme unction
Gospel
Holy Spirit
Old Testament
Priest
Sacrament
Sign of Peace
Viaticum

9.2 THE ADVICE OF JAMES

KEY QUESTION

How does James suggest that the sick were dealt with in the early Church?

CONSULT

James 5:13–15

Extract 1

Is any one of you in trouble? He should pray. Is anyone happy? Let him sing songs of praise. Is any one of you sick? He should call the elders of the church to pray over him and anoint him with oil in the name of the Lord. And the prayer offered in faith will make the sick person well; the Lord will raise him up. If he has sinned he will be forgiven. Therefore confess your sins to each other and pray for each other so that you may be healed. The prayer of a righteous man is powerful and effective.

James 5:13–16

The practice of anointing the sick with oil is one of the sacraments celebrated in the Catholic Church (see 9.1). This sacrament can be traced back to Jesus and his disciples and the evidence for this can be found in one of the Epistles (letters) in the New Testament – the one written by James. This letter, probably written around 50 CE, seems to reflect a practice which was part of the life of the Church from its beginnings.

Healing the sick

James divides the evil that a person may experience in this life into two categories:

1 There are people who suffer hardship as they seek to spread the Gospel message (5:13). This hardship may take the form of persecution, or even death. The people who are afflicted in this way should pray to God for the strength to endure patiently to the end. They should remember that their own lives, and destinies, are in the hands of God. Meanwhile, those who are enjoying a good life at the moment, without any pressure or hardship, should also pray but their prayers should be those of praise to God.

2 Others are suffering physical illness and pain. James tells those who are sick to call on the elders (the presbyters) in their local church to visit them. In Acts 20:28 those chosen to be elders of a church are told to 'shepherd' the people and carry out the work that was later expected of a priest. Two tasks, in particular, are to be carried out:

- **to pray with the sick person.** It is prayer, rather than any action performed, which will bring about their recovery. In the modern Sacrament of the Sick prayer plays a central role, with the priest asking God that his healing and comforting grace might be given to the one in need. Such healing will come through the grace of the Holy Spirit. James is in no doubt that the sick person will be saved by the prayers of the elders: '. . . and the prayer of faith will save the sick person' (5:15).
- **to anoint the person with oil.** The elders were expected to act just like the disciples of Jesus, as described in Mark 6:13. The disciples must have learned the custom of anointing the sick with oil from Jesus himself. We are told that: 'they [the disciples] drove out many demons, and they anointed with oil many who were sick and cured them.' As we saw in 9.1, anointing with oil plays a central role in the service at which the Sacrament of the Sick is performed.

Sin and sickness

James makes an interesting comment about the link between sin and sickness. He did not say that all sickness *can* be traced back to sinful behaviour but that it *might* be. If there is an obvious link in a particular case then the sin needs to be forgiven before the illness can be healed. This is why everyone present at the service for the sick seeks God's forgiveness before the sacrament of anointing begins. This link between sin and suffering, however, makes many people today feel distinctly uncomfortable. What about the person, for example, who is born disabled and has to spend their whole life in a wheelchair? How can one explain the birth of a congenitally deformed child who lives a few short, painful, months? A clear link between sin and sickness leaves too many questions unanswered.

WORK TO DO

1 Read Extract 1 through carefully before answering these questions.
   a) Which sacrament of the Catholic Church is James describing here?
   b) In this sacrament, what is the purpose of praying for someone who is ill and rubbing olive oil on them?
   c) According to James, what is it that will heal the sick person?

2 Explain the link between the advice that James gives in Extract 1 and the Catholic sacrament of anointing the sick.

Extract 2

This text without doubt should be applied to the faithful who are sick and who can be anointed with the holy oil; and this oil, prepared by the bishop, can be used for anointing not only by the priestly hierarchy but by all Christians when they or their dear ones are troubled by sickness.

Innocent I, fifth-century Pope

KEY WORDS

Disciple
Epistle
Holy Spirit
New Testament
Priest
Sacrament

DISCUSSION POINT

What do you think the practice described here by James is intended to bring about – the healing from sickness of a needy person or the giving of God's peace and forgiveness?

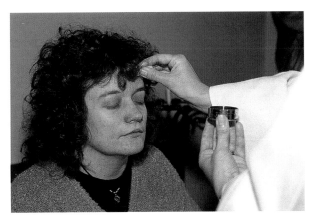

To which group did James entrust the work of visiting and anointing the sick?

In today's world it is the Holy Spirit who brings healing to those in need. Why do you think it is important for Christians to realise this?

9.3 THE HOSPICE MOVEMENT

KEY QUESTION

What is the Hospice Movement and what does it set out to do?

In the Middle Ages hospices were small institutions that looked after the elderly, the sick and travellers. Most of these hospices had a Christian foundation, since the spiritual care of the sick and dying has always been a major task undertaken by the Church. The physical care of the sick and dying has also been undertaken by the religious orders and this has continued in recent years through such devoted workers as Mother Teresa and her Sisters of Charity in India.

The modern Hospice Movement

The modern Hospice Movement began when a group of Irish nuns, the Sisters of Charity, established a home for the dying in Dublin towards the end of the nineteenth century. In 1900 five nuns from this order travelled to London to continue their vocation by caring for the terminally ill in the East End of London. Within a few years they had established the St Joseph's Hospice. Almost sixty years later a young nurse, Cicely Saunders, went to work at St Joseph's. Her nursing career was cut short by a serious back injury, but in 1967 she established the St Christopher's Hospice in London. There are now about 100 in-patient hospices in England offering, at any one time, care for some 2000 patients who are terminally ill. In the USA the first hospice was opened in 1974 and now some 2000 hospices look after more than 300,000 patients.

The aims of the Hospice Movement

Whatever their background, hospices have the same basic objective – to offer care and support for patients, and their friends and relatives, at the most difficult time in their lives. Within this overall objective the Hospice Movement has three main aims:

Extract 1

That those whose lives are diminished or weakened deserve special respect. Sick or handicapped persons should be helped to lead lives as normal as possible . . . Even if death is thought to be imminent, the ordinary care owed to a sick person cannot be legitimately interrupted . . . Palliative care is a special form of disinterested charity. As such it should be encouraged.

CCC (2276, 2279)

1 To relieve pain, whether caused by the illness itself or by the fear and anxiety that the illness causes. Hospices specialise in pain control. Doctors and nurses working in hospices have led the way in palliative care (the control of pain by drugs) in recent years. It is a principle of the Hospice Movement that all pain, no matter how severe it might be, can be brought under control. The CCC (see Extract 1) sees this as an essential element in the care of anyone who is approaching death.

2 To enable patients, friends and relatives to face up to death. Hospices allow them to talk about their fears and anxieties in an open way. Hospices, and those who run them, see this as one of the main reasons for their existence. It is an opportunity that is seldom available in ordinary hospitals. Although most hospices have a Christian foundation no attempt is made to compel people to believe in God. Hospices are open to people of all religious beliefs – and none.

3 To care for the physical and emotional needs of relatives and friends. In modern hospitals the needs of these people are often almost totally forgotten. A hospice seeks to meet those needs.

How hospices help

The demand for bed-space in most hospices is acute and so most of them can only offer fairly short-term care. To begin with, patients often enter for a week or two to give their carers a rest. Then, as their physical condition begins to decline, they are able to enter the hospice for a longer time. At the end of this they can choose whether to die in the hospice or at home. This is an important part of the Hospice philosophy. It leaves the patient with a real measure of independence and yet, if they choose to die at home, they still have access to the facilities of the hospice. Macmillan Nurses, who specialise in the care of those with cancer, are attached to many hospices. The emphasis is very much on death with dignity, wherever that death takes place.

WORK TO DO

1 How did the modern Hospice Movement begin?

2 What is distinctive about the kind of care that is provided by the modern Hospice Movement?

3 What does a hospice set out to achieve?

4 In what ways do the Church and individual Christians offer help to those who are terminally ill?

5 'It would be better to spend money on people who have a chance of living rather than on those who are dying.' Do you agree? Give reasons for your answer.

6 In Extract 1 the CCC describes palliative care of the dying as 'a special form of disinterested charity'.
   a) What is palliative care?
   b) Why do you think that the CCC describes it as 'a special form of disinterested charity'?

DISCUSSION POINT

'Hospices do such important work in looking after those who are dying that they should be financed, and supported, by the State.' Do you agree with this comment?

KEY WORDS
Hospice
Vocation

In this hospice, run by Roman Catholic nuns, prayer and meditation is offered to those who want it. What part do you think these religious practices could play in the life of a person who is approaching death?

9.4 DEATH – AND BEYOND (1)

KEY QUESTION

How does the Roman Catholic Church deal with death?

Extract 1

Life is given us that we may learn to die well, and we never think of it. To die well we must live well.

St John Vianney

Extract 2

The Church who, as Mother, has borne the Christian sacramentally in her womb during his earthly pilgrimage, accompanies him at his journey's end, in order to surrender him 'into the Father's hands'. She offers to the Father, in Christ, the child of his grace, and she commits to the earth, in hope, the seed of the body that will rise in glory.

CCC (1683)

Death is the only certainty in life and it constantly overshadows everything that we do. It is the teaching of the Catholic Church that there is a very close link between life and death (see Extract 1). According to this teaching, death is:

- a constant reminder to human beings that they are all mortal and that all life ends.
- the completion of all human actions and choices.

Both of these aspects are reflected in the way that death is dealt with in the rituals and teachings of the Roman Catholic Church. These rituals set out to encourage mourners to look back and be thankful for the life that they are celebrating and to look beyond death to eternal life. Just as Jesus rose from the dead after three days, so all Christians believe that they, too, will rise from the dead to spend eternity with God. As the Creed says: 'I believe . . . in the resurrection of the body and life everlasting.' You will find out more about this belief in life after death in 9.5.

The funeral Mass

The Church says farewell to someone who has died in three stages:

1 In the home. Often an all-night vigil or 'wake' is held in the home as relatives and friends take turns to 'watch over' the body.

2 In church. The coffin is often taken to the church on the night before the funeral Mass and placed in front of the altar. The Mass itself begins with the priest greeting mourners and the coffin at the door of the church. He sprinkles the coffin with holy water as a reminder that the dead person was incorporated into the death and resurrection of Jesus when they were baptised. Often a white pall, recalling the white robe of baptism, is placed on the coffin before the procession moves forward. The service continues with the Mass. This begins, as always, with the Liturgy of the Word before moving on to the Liturgy of the Eucharist. At the conclusion of the Mass, after a moment of silent prayer, the coffin is again sprinkled with holy water and incense. The final commendation of the body to God emphasises the shared hope

How do you think a Christian might draw strength from the death of Jesus as he or she approaches death?

Why do you think that the coffin is often left in a church on the night before it is buried?

of all Christians in life after death because of the death and resurrection of Jesus.

Funeral Masses are not allowed during the Tridium (Holy Thursday, Good Friday and the Easter Vigil). They are not permitted, either, on the holy days of obligation or on the Sundays of Advent, Lent or Easter. Simple burial services, however, are allowed during these times.

3 At the graveside or in the crematorium. The Catholic Church does not express any strong preference for burial or cremation. The prayers which are said around the graveside insist on the final hope which every Christian has, whilst, at the same time, recognising the heartache of relatives and friends.

As we shall see in 9.5, the way in which the Catholic Church deals with death reflects the beliefs that it holds about heaven, purgatory and hell.

WORK TO DO

1 a) In the time between the death of a person and their burial, ceremonies take place in three different places. What are these places?
   b) Why do you think that the Catechism of the Catholic Church insists that it is important that each of these places is included in the funeral rites?

2 Describe the main features of a Catholic funeral. Explain how the funeral, combined with what goes before and after, reflects what a Roman Catholic believes about life after death. In your answer you may refer to:
   a) the preparations for the service
   b) the funeral Mass
   c) the burial or cremation.

DISCUSSION POINT

How is the Roman Catholic ritual intended to provide help and reassurance for the friends and relatives of the person who has died?

Extract 3

It is in the face of death that the riddle of human existence becomes most acute . . . Although the mystery of death utterly beggars the imagination, the Church has been taught by divine revelation, and herself firmly teaches, that man has been created by God for a blissful purpose beyond the reach of human misery.

The Second Vatican Council

KEY WORDS

Advent
Altar
Creed
Easter
Easter Vigil
Good Friday
Lent
Liturgy of the Eucharist
Liturgy of the Word
Mass
Priest
Purgatory
Sunday
Tridium

9.5 DEATH – AND BEYOND (2)

KEY QUESTION

What does the Catholic Church teach about judgement and life after death?

CONSULT

Matthew 25:31–46;
Luke 16:19–31

Extract 1

For all of us must appear before Christ, to be judged by him. We will each receive what we deserve, according to everything we have done, good or bad, in our bodily life.

2 Corinthians 5:10

Catholics, like all Christians, believe that Jesus rose from the dead. What comfort do you think this might give someone who is mourning the loss of a loved one?

Death is the beginning of eternal life. It is the moment when the eternal soul is separated from the body. The book of Ecclesiastes says that death is perfectly natural: 'There is a season for everything . . . a time for giving birth and a time for dying.' (3:1–2).

The particular judgement

The Catholic Church believes that all people appear before God immediately after death for a 'particular judgement'. This gives either entrance into heaven (immediately or after purification in purgatory) or into the eternal punishment of hell. Jesus described this judgement in his parable of Lazarus and the rich man (Luke 16:19–31). On earth, the rich man ignored the starving Lazarus but, after death, he was sent to hell whilst Lazarus went to a place of eternal happiness. The same teaching is found in the parable of the sheep and the goats (see 3.4) in which all people are divided into two distinct groups – one destined for hell (the goats) and the other heading for heaven (the sheep).

The Second Coming

The general ('last') judgement will take place at the end of time, when Jesus returns to earth as its judge. This event, the Second Coming, will be very different from the first coming of Jesus when he was born as a baby in Bethlehem. At the Second Coming (called the Parousia) Jesus, with his angels, will return to earth in great glory and power. When this happens every true believer will recognise Jesus as their Lord and Master.

The Church looks forward to this future event every year during the liturgical season of Advent. During the four weeks of Advent, leading up to Christmas, Roman Catholics prepare themselves to celebrate the first coming of Jesus – and his Second Coming. They look forward to both events with great anticipation. The season of Advent is a reminder to all Catholics that Jesus is with them now, through his Holy Spirit, and will return at the end of time to begin a new order which will last for eternity.

After judgement

The parable of the sheep and the goats (see above) is a reminder that the way people live in this life determines where they spend eternity. The teaching of the Church speaks of three different destinations after death and judgement. One is temporary and two are permanent:

1 Heaven The reward for those who are perfect in love is to see God as he is. Catholics call this 'the beatific vision'. Catholics believe that Jesus, by his death, opened up heaven for all true believers, where there will be: '. . . no more death, no more grief or dying or pain. The old things have disappeared.' (Revelation 21:4). Heaven is the name for a life lived in eternal communion with God, the Virgin Mary, the angels and the saints.

2 Purgatory Few people are pure enough to enter heaven directly when they die. For the vast majority a time of purification and cleansing is needed. The Church believes that making intercession (praying) for those in purgatory can shorten their stay there. Intercession can be made through indulgences, penance, almsgiving and prayers. In the Church calendar the month of November is set aside to pray for those in purgatory.

3 Hell For those who reject God's love there is a very heavy price to pay. Hell is eternal separation from God. Jesus spoke more than once of hell as a place of great torment (see Mark 9:47–48). The existence of hell should impel the Church to work even harder for the salvation of every sinner.

WORK TO DO

1 St Athanasius was a church leader in the third century. He agreed that people naturally fear death but those who put their faith in Jesus despise what they naturally fear.
   a) What do you think it is about death that people most fear?
   b) How do you think that faith in Jesus might help to lessen that fear?

2 Describe the teaching of the Catholic Church on:
   a) heaven
   b) purgatory
   c) hell.

3 Imagine that you are helping a friend to come to terms with a bereavement. What teachings of the Catholic Church would you stress to help them?

Extract 2

All who die in God's grace and friendship, but still imperfectly purified, are indeed assured of their eternal salvation; but after death they undergo purification, so as to achieve the holiness necessary to enter the joy of heaven. The Church gives the name 'Purgatory' to this final purification of the elect . . .

CCC (1030–31)

DISCUSSION POINT

What are your own beliefs about life, death, hell, purgatory and heaven?

KEY WORDS

Advent
Almsgiving
Holy Spirit
Indulgence
Parable
Penance
Purgatory
Second Coming
Virgin Mary

Catholics believe in a 'particular' and a 'general' resurrection of the dead. What is the difference between them?

9.6 RESPECT FOR HUMAN LIFE

KEY QUESTION

What does the Roman Catholic Church teach about the uniqueness and value of human life?

Extract 1

Then God said, 'Let us make man in our image, in our likeness, and let them rule over the fish of the sea and birds of the air, over the livestock, all over the earth, and over all the creatures that move along the ground. God created man in his own image, in the image of God he created him: male and female he created them.'

Genesis 1:26,27

What similarity do you think human beings bear to their Creator?

The CCC teaches clearly that it is the vocation of human beings to live their lives in the light and by the power of the Holy Spirit. This is essentially what makes human beings different from all other forms of life. Human beings have a spiritual dimension and capacity which other forms of life do not possess. This means that they are the only creatures to have a 'soul' and it is this spiritual dimension which is able to respond to God.

Made in the image of God

The dignity of human beings stems from their creation in the image of God, as you can see from Extract 1. The book of Genesis ('beginnings') teaches clearly that all other forms of life were created before human beings. We are told that, after each stage of creation, God looked at what he had done and 'saw that it was good'. Nothing, though, is said to have been made in the divine image until the first man and woman. Both of them bore a striking spiritual similarity to their Creator.

This similarity, though, was disfigured by the Fall, through which sin entered the world. The divine image in human beings was restored when Christ came as Redeemer and Saviour and is now present in everyone (see Extract 2). It can be seen in the unity that people enjoy with each other, which reflects that unity which the members of the Trinity have with each other. Endowed with a 'spiritual and immortal soul' the human being alone is set aside for eternal communion with God. It is in this that the true uniqueness of human beings lies.

Human beings struggle

Human beings also have the free will which allows them to live lives that are pleasing to God. Through the Holy Spirit they are able to understand, and follow, the path that God wants them to follow. God makes this path clear through the conscience, which is another uniquely human faculty. At the same time, though, human beings still carry the wound of original sin (see 7.8). Humankind is still prone to evil and subject to giving in to sinful desires. The struggle against sin is a constant battle. It can only be successful because, by his death on the cross, Jesus delivered all believers from Satan and from sin. As the ccc puts it: 'His grace restores what sin has damaged in us' (1708).

The implications

The implications of these beliefs about the uniqueness of human beings are immense. If all human beings are created in the image of God then everyone must be equal. No one group can treat another as inferior. All forms of racism and sexism, therefore, are immoral. The conception and birth of each new life is down to God alone, as is the welfare of that person from conception through to death. The moment when each person dies, and eternity begins, is a matter for divine, and not human, decision.

Whatever a person's age, state of health, educational achievements, intelligence level or place in society, their contribution to life is always extremely valuable. Their value, and importance, is God-given and cannot be taken away. Their life should not be terminated, under any circumstances. A discussion about the morality of abortion can be found in 9.7 and 9.8. Equally importantly, Roman Catholics are totally opposed to any practice linked or associated with euthanasia. A full discussion about the morality of ending a person's life prematurely through artificial means can be found in 9.9. At the beginning of the twenty-first century both of these practices have become increasingly important moral and spiritual issues.

WORK TO DO

1 a) Write down three reasons why Catholics believe that all human life is sacred.
   b) What do you understand by the word 'sacred' here?

2 How do Roman Catholics believe that human beings are different from other forms of life?

3 Why do Roman Catholics believe that all forms of human life should be protected?

4 a) What does the Catholic Church mean when it says that it is always on the side of human life?
   b) Describe two areas of life in which this principle might be applied.

The divine image in each person was partially lost through the Fall. How was it restored by the death of Jesus?

Extract 2

It is in Christ, Redeemer and Saviour, that the divine image, disfigured in man by the first sin, has been restored to its original beauty and ennobled by the grace of God.

CCC (1701)

DISCUSSION POINT

What do you think the Bible means when it says that God created man 'in his own image'?

KEY WORDS

Abortion
Euthanasia
Fall
Holy Spirit
Original Sin
Satan
Trinity
Vocation

9.7 ABORTION (1)

KEY QUESTION

What changes did the 1967 Abortion Act make in Britain?

The word 'abortion' can be applied to two different situations:
- an abortion is the deliberate killing of an unborn human being by using a medical or a surgical procedure.
- a 'spontaneous abortion' is known as a miscarriage and is the expulsion of the foetus from the womb without any artificial means being used. It is thought that about 25 per cent of all pregnancies end in miscarriage, usually but not always within the first 12 weeks of pregnancy.

In this unit we are looking at abortion in the first sense. If there is any moral teaching in the Catholic Church which is absolute (binding in all situations) it is its teaching about abortion. Abortion has been condemned in every age of the Church. Successive Popes, Church Councils and bishops have taught that abortion is indefensible since the unborn child is innocent of any offence and incapable of defending itself. Abortion is a mortal sin and those people involved in arranging it or co-operating with it should be punished by excommunication from the sacraments of the Church.

Extract 1

The child, by reason of its physical and mental immaturity, needs special safeguards and care, including appropriate legal protection, before as well as after birth.

United Nations Declaration on Human Rights

Abortion legalised

Before 1967 abortion was illegal in Britain. However, large numbers (around 200,000 a year) of 'back-street' abortions were carried out by unqualified people. Performed in squalid conditions, these abortions frequently led to the serious injury or death of the mother. Thousands of women were made infertile, and in the years leading up to 1967 about 60 women died each year as a result of these illegal operations.

In 1967, the Abortion Act was passed by Parliament to put an end to this unfortunate situation. It made abortion legal, providing that:
- two registered doctors agree that an abortion can legally be carried out.
- it is carried out before 'the time of viability', i.e. the time when the baby can exist on its own outside its mother's womb. This was originally set at 28 weeks (seven months) of pregnancy but this was reduced to 24 weeks in 1990.
- continuing the pregnancy would involve a greater risk to the mother, or any existing child in the family, than terminating the pregnancy.
- a termination is necessary to prevent permanent physical or emotional damage to the mother.
- there is a real risk that the baby will be born physically disabled or with learning difficulties.

Extract 2

From the time the ovum is fertilised, a life is begun which is neither that of the father or mother. It is the life of a new human being with its own growth. It would never become human if it was not human already.

Roman Catholic Declaration on procured abortion, 1974

Abortion on demand?

Opponents of abortion argue that the Abortion Act has virtually created 'abortion on demand', i.e. abortion without any real restrictions. Those who support abortion say that the 1967 Act confronted the realities of the situation, since thousands of illegal abortions were carried out before 1967, often with very serious consequences. In 1968 157,000 terminations were carried out. By 1990 this figure had risen to 173,900 but the numbers then started to decline. In 1990 the Committee on Safety of Medicines declared that there was an increased risk of thrombosis for women taking seven brands of contraceptive pill. Many women stopped using the Pill and this led to an increase in the number of conceptions and a consequent rise in the number of abortions.

About 20 per cent of all abortions in Britain are performed on women from outside the country, especially from Spain and the Republic of Ireland (Eire), where abortion is illegal. About 18 per cent (one in six) of all pregnancies now end in abortion. The largest increase in abortions since 1968 has been amongst women in the 16–19 age group. One in every 40 women in this group now has an abortion each year.

WORK TO DO

1 a) What is an abortion?
  b) Why was it considered necessary to introduce the Abortion Act in 1967?
  c) What does the Abortion Act say about abortion?
  d) What is 'abortion on demand'?
  e) Do you think that the 1967 Abortion Act amounts to a licence for abortion on demand?

2 a) What are your own feelings about abortion? Set them down as clearly as you can and support them by argument.
  b) Explain how important the Roman Catholic Church, has been in forming your opinions about abortion.

DISCUSSION POINT

How would you recognise a life lived by the virtues of Do you think that Roman Catholics who have an abortion, or are involved in carrying out abortions, should be punished by the Church?

KEY WORDS

Abortion
Bishop
Church Council
Pope
Sacrament

What do you think that this sculpture of the hands of God holding a baby has to say about abortion?

9.8 ABORTION (2)

KEY QUESTION

Why is the Roman Catholic Church absolutely opposed to abortion?

Most Roman Catholics today agree that to directly end the life of a foetus in the womb is a serious moral sin. From the earliest times the tradition of the Catholic Church has been against abortion and infanticide – the ancient practice of killing young children. The Didache, which dates from the early second century, teaches that 'You shall not kill a child by abortion, nor kill it at birth'. Various Church documents over the centuries have linked abortion and infanticide and roundly condemned both of them as being immoral.

Abortion probably raises stronger emotions than any other moral issue. In the USA, for instance, opponents of abortion have from time to time burned down clinics and murdered doctors held responsible for carrying out the operations. To understand the depth of emotion felt on this issue we must look at the arguments for (pro-choice) and against (pro-life) abortion.

Extract 1

Life must be protected with the utmost care from the moment of conception. Abortion and infanticide are abominable crimes.

Gaudium et Spes, *Second Vatican Council*

Extract 2

All human life is sacred. All men must recognise this fact.

Humanae Vitae, *Pope Paul VI*

Arguments for legal abortion

- Each woman has the right to choose what happens to her own body. The foetus is part of that body until the time when it is able to survive independently on its own. The law recognises this by making abortion available up to the time of 'viability' (24 weeks). In practice, though, few abortions are carried out after 18 weeks and the vast majority are performed before 14 weeks.
- Every child has the right to be born into a loving family which can meet its material and emotional needs. If basic care cannot be provided then an abortion is justified. There are too many unwanted babies in the world – why add to them?
- Other members of a pregnant woman's family also have rights. This includes the woman's partner and other children. If the woman discovers that her baby will be disabled then she has the right to decide whether she, and the family, can cope. If not, then an abortion is the only possible solution.
- A woman who becomes pregnant after being raped should not be compelled to carry her attacker's baby. The child would be a constant reminder to her of that act of violence.

Arguments against abortion

- Every child is a precious, and unique, gift from God. No one can have the right to destroy that gift. This rule is absolute and even covers the case of a woman who has been raped.
- Every baby is defenceless and needs protecting. The rights of the unborn child are at least equal to those of the mother – if they don't exceed them.
- An embryo is a human being from the moment it is conceived, since it goes on to grow into a full human being. This is as true of someone who is disabled from birth as it is of the able-bodied.
- Abortion places an intolerable burden on doctors and nurses, many of whom may have serious moral and religious objections to abortion. In any case the Hippocratic Oath, which all doctors sign, compels them to save life – not to destroy it.

Clearly much of the debate about abortion centres around the unresolved issue of just when life begins. Pro-life groups such as the Society for the Protection of the Unborn Child (SPUC) and LIFE, which draw much of their support from Roman Catholics, argue that life begins when the ovum and sperm fuse (see Extract 3). Others maintain that human life, as we know it, begins at some time during pregnancy – probably when the baby is developed enough to survive on its own outside the womb. There are those, however, who maintain strongly that human life does not really begin until a baby is born and becomes truly independent from its mother.

WORK TO DO

1 'No Christian should ever consider having an abortion.' Do you agree with this statement?

2 The Roman Catholic Church teaches that abortion is wrong in every conceivable situation.
   a) What are the main reasons put forward by the Church for holding this position?
   b) Is this a point of view that you feel comfortable with? Explain your answer.

3 The Roman Catholic Church believes that the rights of the unborn child are at least equal to those of the mother. Do you think that this position is right?

4 a) What are the main arguments for abortion?
   b) What are the main arguments against abortion?

Extract 3

Human life must be respected and protected absolutely from the moment of conception. From the first moment of his existence a human being must be recognised as having the rights of a person – among which is the inviolable right of every innocent human being to life . . . Abortion and infanticide are abominable crimes . . . The law must provide appropriate penal sanctions for every deliberate violation of the child's rights.

CCC (2270)

DISCUSSION POINT

The Roman Catholic Church believes that it is wrong to take life at any time. Even a woman who has been raped or is expecting a disabled child should not have an abortion. What do you think?

KEY WORD
Abortion

The Roman Catholic Church teaches that life begins at conception. Do you agree with this view?

9.9 EUTHANASIA

KEY QUESTION

What is euthanasia and why is the Catholic Church so strongly opposed to it?

According to the Vatican Declaration on Euthanasia (1980) euthanasia is: 'an action or an omission which of itself or by intention causes death, in order that all suffering may in this way be eliminated'. The word itself means 'easy death' and it raises very strong emotions because it goes to the very heart of what people believe about life and death. It is important, though, to draw a clear distinction between:

- compulsory euthanasia, as used by fascist governments such as the Nazis in the Second World War, and morally indefensible. Nobody would seriously argue for this today.
- voluntary euthanasia, available for those who want it when their lives become intolerable.

It is this second form of euthanasia that lies at the heart of the current debate.

Extract 1

The argument for euthanasia would be met if medical skill in terminal care is improved, pre-death loneliness is relieved, patient and family are supported by the statutory services and the family. The whole of a patient's needs, including the spiritual, must be met.

Methodist Conference, 1974

Arguments for legal euthanasia

There are many who argue that everyone has the right to choose to make a dignified exit from this life. The Voluntary Euthanasia Society, now called EXIT, has argued for this for a long time:

- Faced with a terminal illness, for which there is no possible cure, everyone should be able to enjoy 'the mercy of a painless death'. This is a basic human right.
- If a person requests it then a doctor should be able to assist them to end their own life. A 'living will' can be made when a person is healthy, stipulating that their life should not be artificially prolonged at any time.
- As a safeguard the request for euthanasia should have been signed at least 30 days before it is carried out.
- A person is saving relatives and friends from the unnecessary suffering and anguish brought about by seeing their loved one dying in pain. They are also saving scarce medical resources which could be used to help those who might be cured.

Extract 2

Anything which says to the very ill that they are a burden to their family and that they would be better off dead is unacceptable. What sort of society could let its old folk die because they are 'in the way'?

Dr Cicely Saunders, founder of the modern hospice movement

Arguments against euthanasia

The Roman Catholic Church, and almost all other Churches, have come out strongly against any form of euthanasia:

- There are now ways in which pain can be controlled and people can die with dignity. The modern Hospice Movement is built on the premise that pain can be controlled to the end – a branch of medicine known as 'palliative care'. The downside to this is that there are comparatively few hospices in the country.
- Only God has the right to decide when a person should die. Human beings, unlike any other form of life, have eternal souls which are in the safe keeping of God. It is improper, therefore, for anyone to decide the moment of their death. This is one of the reasons why the Catholic Church has always condemned suicide, since no one has the right to take their own life. Euthanasia and suicide are forms of murder – an act expressly forbidden by the Ten Commandments.
- Doctors take the Hippocratic Oath when they qualify and this binds them to 'do everything possible to preserve and restore life and not to take it'. Taking active steps to end a person's life is plainly against the meaning and the spirit of this Oath.

- People sometimes recover even when all hope seems to be gone.
- There is a world of difference between discontinuing treatment and actively killing someone. The CCC offers the following guideline on this: 'Discontinuing medical procedures that are burdensome, dangerous, extraordinary or disproportionate to the expected outcome can be legitimate' (CCC 2278).

The Catholic Church accepts that any treatment which, at best, can prolong a life for only a short time need not be given if the patient is opposed to it. Some treatments which offer this brief respite, such as chemotherapy in cancer cases, are painful with very unpleasant side effects.

WORK TO DO

1 a) What does the word 'euthanasia' mean?
   b) What is the difference between voluntary and compulsory euthanasia?
   c) Why do Christians disagree amongst themselves about euthanasia?

2 Explain why some Christians want voluntary euthanasia to be made legal in this country.

3 a) What are two of the main arguments in favour of euthanasia?
   b) What are two of the main arguments against euthanasia?

4 Do you think that there are some situations in which euthanasia might be right? Describe two such situations.

DISCUSSION POINT

'It is God who gives life in the first place and he alone should take it away.' Do you agree with this argument? What relevance do you think it has to the discussion on euthanasia?

KEY WORDS

Euthanasia
Hospice
Ten Commandments

Extract 3

The use of painkillers to alleviate the suffering of the dying, even at the risk of shortening their days, can be morally in conformity with human dignity if death is not to be willed either as an end or a means, but only foreseen and tolerated as inevitable.

CCC (2279)

How do you think that society can convey the message to elderly people that they are wanted and valued to the end?

10 WORK AND LEISURE

10.1 WORK

KEY QUESTION

Why is work so important to human beings?

In the UK there are about 26 million people in paid employment, and for them work is a natural part of their lives, as well as the means of providing for themselves and their families. It is tempting, therefore, simply to define work as: 'any activity for which we are paid'. Tempting but inaccurate. Many 'leisure' activities, such as working out in a gym or running a marathon, are extremely hard work but are unpaid. So, too, are the unpaid hours spent on housework, or caring for children or other dependent relatives. Work, therefore, needs to be defined as: 'any meaningful or purposeful activity which a person does, whether he or she is paid for it or not'.

Extract 1

Then I realised that it is good and proper for a man to eat and drink, and to find satisfaction in his toilsome labour under the sun during the few days of life God has given him – for this is his lot. Moreover, when God gives any man wealth and possessions, and enables him to enjoy them, to accept his lot and be happy in his work – this is a gift of God.

Ecclesiastes 5:19

Extract 2

Everyone has the right to work and to just and favourable conditions of employment. Everyone has the right to equal pay for equal work. Everyone has the right to form and join a trade union.

United Nations Declaration on Human Rights

Why do people work?

- **To satisfy basic needs** The first man was given work to do so that he could survive: 'The Lord God took the man and put him in the Garden of Eden to till it and look after it' (Genesis 2:15). Human beings need food and shelter in order to survive, and in Western societies people work to satisfy these basic needs. They also work to satisfy their 'wants' for more material security. In many developing countries, though, wages barely meet the basic needs of the family and everyone is involved in the never-ending struggle to stay alive.

- **To achieve personal satisfaction and self-respect** Work is an essential part of being human. For most people, their sense of identity and self-worth are closely linked to their occupation. This is why so many people go through an 'identity crisis' if they suddenly lose their job and become unemployed (see 10.2).

- **To find a sense of achievement and fulfilment** For many people, work simply means boredom and drudgery. For others, however, it brings real satisfaction. Christians believe that any job, no matter how mundane, should be done to the glory of God.

- **To bring us into contact with other people** Most people need to interact with their colleagues in a busy work environment. Only a few people, such as artists and writers, are happy working without day-to-day contact with others.

Christians and work

The Bible has a great deal to say about work and its importance in individual lives. From the story of creation in Genesis 1 and 2 we discover that God worked intensively for six days but rested on the seventh. God blessed the day of rest and made it a holy day (Genesis 2:3) and from this developed the Jewish Sabbath Day. Once the first man and woman had been expelled from the Garden of Eden, hard work became a necessity to tame the earth and make it productive (Genesis 3:17–19). A person could be lazy if they wished but if they were, they would go hungry (Proverbs 19:15).

Paul takes up the same idea. As a travelling preacher, Paul earned his living by making tents, so that he was not a financial burden on anyone (2 Thessalonians 3:8). He passed on to others a simple rule of thumb: 'If a man will not work, he shall not eat.' Every piece of work, whatever it is, is to be carried out to the glory of God, whether it wins the praise of employers or not (Ephesians 6:5–8). Work should be an act of service to others, for which a person should not expect to win human praise (Mark 10:43). Those unable to work should always remember that God looks after the birds and the flowers, without them having to work (Matthew 6:26–29).

WORK TO DO

1 a) What is the Christian ideal of work?
   b) Do you think that it is possible to live up to this ideal in the modern world?

2 Why do you think that work is so important?

3 'Work is simply a means of earning enough money to live, nothing else.' Do you agree with this summary of the purpose and value of work?

4 Why might a Christian think that it is important to have a job?

Extract 3

> Whatever you do, work at it with all your heart, as working for the Lord, not for men, since you know that you will receive an inheritance from the Lord as a reward.

Colossians 3:23,24

Why do you think that having a job, and working, means so much to these people?

DISCUSSION POINT

What responsibilities do you think employers and employees have to each other in the world of work?

KEY WORDS

Paul
Sabbath Day

KEY QUESTION

What are the main causes of unemployment?

For most of the early 1990s the number of people unemployed in the UK exceeded 2 million. Then, in 1993, the figure began to decline and it continued to go down for the remainder of the century. By the beginning of the year 2000 it was around one million. It is thought that there will always be at least 500,000 people who are 'unemployable' – through physical or mental incapacity. Christians believe that helping those in need in society must include giving practical help to those without work.

The causes of unemployment

The problem of unemployment in the UK in recent years has been brought about by a combination of factors:

- A decline in heavy and manufacturing industries in the 1970s and 1980s. For example, many mines closed during this period and thousands of miners lost their jobs. Power stations and other heavy users of coal found that they could import coal more cheaply from Poland and other eastern European countries.
- A considerable increase in mechanisation and automation took place within manufacturing and service industries (particularly banking and insurance). This is a trend which will certainly continue well into the foreseeable future. This trend has led to many people losing their jobs.
- A growth in the number of people seeking work, especially women seeking a return to work, since the 1960s. The 'working mother' is a much more common phenomenon than she used to be. As a result more and more people are chasing fewer and fewer jobs.

Problems caused by unemployment

- Low morale, depression and poor self-esteem amongst the unemployed, even leading, in a few cases, to suicide. Obviously, these problems increase the longer that unemployment lasts.
- Tensions within a family leading, in many cases, to a breakdown in family life. There is a strong link between unemployment and divorce.
- An increase in drug-taking and alcohol abuse. As the money to finance these addictions is not available so the levels of robbery and theft increase in their wake.
- An increase in criminal behaviour and typical inner-city problems such as vandalism, violence and even rioting.
- An increase in racial attacks and abuse. People who are angry at having lost their jobs often look around for 'scapegoats' to blame. Those from the ethnic minorities sometimes find themselves under fire.

Unemployment is rarely the sole cause of these social problems. It does, however, give people much more spare time than they would normally have and this can lead to a sharp increase in various forms of social and personal misbehaviour. Unemployment usually leads to irritation, frustration and despair, which can often spill over into anti-social behaviour, especially amongst young people.

Extract 1

Unemployment almost always wounds its victim's dignity and threatens the equilibrium of his life. Besides the harm done to him personally, it entails many risks for his family.

CCC (2436)

Unemployed workers in Africa. Do you think that unemployment, or under-employment, causes the same problems wherever it is found?

The Church and unemployment

Although unemployment does tend to be highest in urban areas, it is a problem which now affects every part of the country. The Church is about the only organisation which is present in almost all levels of society. It is inevitable, therefore, that the Church should find itself involved in working amongst those who are the victims of unemployment. In many places it:

- runs counselling and training centres to help the unemployed to find work
- provides food and clothing for those without any regular source of income
- sets up schemes to help people use their enforced leisure time constructively
- runs 'job clubs' to encourage and help the unemployed to find work.

WORK TO DO

1 What are the main:
   a) personal
   b) social
   problems caused by widespread unemployment?

2 'No matter what country we live in, rich or poor, we all have the right to expect to have a job.' What do you think a Christian might say to support this particular point of view?

3 Read 2 Thessalonians 3:6–11.
   a) What did Paul have to say about people who would not work?
   b) Do you agree with his opinion?
   c) Do you think that his words have any relevance today?

4 Why might a Christian think that it is very important to have a job?

Extract 2

> Unemployment is the worst evil, in the sense that the unemployed feel that they have fallen out of common life . . . they are not wanted, that is the thing that has the power to corrupt the soul of any man.

William Temple, Archbishop of Canterbury, 1942–44

DISCUSSION POINT

Imagine that you are in your mid-thirties, married and with two children. What effect do you think a prolonged spell of unemployment might have on you and other people in your family?

10.3 LEISURE

KEY QUESTION

What is leisure and why is it so important to human well-being?

Many people look forward to retirement as a time when they can pursue their own interests. Others dread retiring. Why do you think this is?

Extract 1

Everyone has the right to rest and leisure, including reasonable working hours and holidays with pay.

United Nations Declaration on Human Rights

The statement in the United Nations Declaration on Human Rights (see Extract 1) follows the standard first laid down in the Old Testament (see Extract 2). From the very beginning of their history the Jews maintained that a day of rest, the Sabbath Day, had been ordained by God as the day on which all work should stop. Just as God had rested on the seventh day from creating the world, so Jews were to rest from all of their work on this day as well.

This Biblical principle was underlining something that modern people have gradually come to realise – that a balanced life must include elements of work, rest and play. The person who works impossibly long hours – a 'workaholic' – will end up suffering from stress and anxiety. The person who rests all the time will be denied the stimulation and enjoyment that creative work can bring. A balanced combination of work and leisure is in the interests of everyone.

The ages of leisure

Whilst our leisure interests and activities change as we get older it seems that most of us pass through five distinct 'ages of leisure'.

1 **The childhood/teenage phase**   This time is mainly spent playing and being with our friends, taking part in sport, computer activities or watching TV.

2 **Early married life (twenties and early thirties)**   Leisure activities centre around a new home, bringing up children, DIY and indoor hobbies. Opportunities to go out are severely limited and so are highly valued.

3 **Early middle age (35–45)**   As the children grow up, so people are free to spend more time outside the home with friends, eating out, and becoming involved with church and other group activities.

4 **Later middle age (45–65)**   Once the children have left home parents are free to pursue interests such as golf and bridge and to take longer holidays.

5 **Old age (65 onwards)**   Leisure activities are likely to be less physical, with knitting, gardening, walking and playing with grandchildren amongst the most popular leisure activities.

Most people today have far more leisure time than their ancestors did a century ago. The average working week is about 37 hours, while in 1900 it was twice as long. Statistics like these, though, can be very misleading. Mothers with young children or those caring for aged or disabled relatives can have little free time. Moreover, the whole idea of leisure is meaningless to those people in developing countries who are involved in a life or death struggle for survival.

Christians and leisure

Christians believe that leisure, like work, is an opportunity to serve God. There are some activities which are acceptable to God and others which are not. Christians sometimes disagree, though, over what falls into each category. There is a strong 'temperance' tradition, especially in the **Salvation Army** and the **Methodist Church**, which emphasises the dangers of drinking alcohol. Gambling, a popular leisure pursuit, is also condemned by both Churches.

The parable of the talents (Matthew 25:14–30) suggests that everyone is given different talents by God. They have been given these talents so that they can develop them and use them to benefit other people. Leisure time provides the ideal opportunity for these talents to be developed and used. Whether the talent lies in artistic, sporting or other areas it can almost certainly be used for the enjoyment and benefit of other people. To do this in one's free time would, in Christian eyes, be an extremely good use of one's leisure time.

WORK TO DO

1 Read Extract 1.
   a) Do you think that everyone has the 'right' to enjoy reasonable leisure time?
   b) How would you define 'reasonable working hours' and 'holidays with pay' in the UK today?

2 a) What is leisure?
   b) Why do you think that leisure time is so important in the modern world?
   c) What do you think is a 'good' use of leisure time?
   d) What do you think would be a 'bad' use of leisure time?

3 Do you think it matters how Christians use their leisure time? Give reasons for your answer.

4 Do you think that it is a pity that Sunday has become a day on which people can do the same things that they do on the other six days of the week?

Extract 2

Remember to keep the Sabbath Day holy. You have six days to labour and do all your work; but the seventh day is a sabbath of the Lord your God . . . for in six days the Lord made the heavens and the earth, the sea and all that is in them, and on the seventh day he rested. Therefore the Lord blessed the Sabbath Day and declared it holy.

Exodus 8:11

DISCUSSION POINT

It is ironic that people in this country are working longer hours than they did ten years ago. Do you think there is a hidden danger in this trend?

KEY WORDS

Methodist Church
Old Testament
Sabbath Day
Salvation Army

Why do you think that the vast majority of parents look upon the time that they spend with their children as time very well spent?

11 VOCATION

11.1 WHAT IS A VOCATION?

KEY QUESTION

What is a vocation and how has this been understood in the Roman Catholic Church?

Extract 1

In the New Testament Jesus called his followers to build the Kingdom of God by way of discipleship, by living the Gospel values; later on some of Jesus' followers were calling others to serve the Church, to minister to one another in preaching, teaching or healing. All were called to follow Jesus on their way to the Father. Each one of us has been given a similar call to follow the Lord and to use our gifts and talents for each other in making God's kingdom of love, truth, peace and justice, present on earth in our time. We are called to follow Christ in various ways – as married or single persons, as priests or religious.

The National Religious Vocation Centre

The word 'vocation' comes from the Latin *vocare* which means 'to call'. This provides us with the root meaning of the word which has been used in the Catholic Church for centuries in two distinct ways:

1 A common vocation. The three Sacraments of Initiation – Baptism, Confirmation and Holy Communion – call all Christians to a life of holiness, to be servants and witnesses to the Gospel of God. They give all believers the grace that they need to lead Christ-like lives in the service of others. Furthermore, through baptism and confirmation, each of us is initiated into the common priesthood of all believers. All are members of the Body of Christ, the Church, and so have a part to play in the growth of that Body on earth.

The idea of the priesthood of all believers is an important Roman Catholic doctrine and needs some explanation here. Jesus is the supreme mediator between God and people and the priest continues this work of mediation as he dispenses the Sacraments, especially the Eucharist. When we are joined to Jesus in baptism we, too, share in his priestly function, although certain responsibilities remain the prerogative of an ordained priest. Ordinary believers are involved in God's work of salvation in the world in a variety of different ways:
- through prayer
- through the loving service of others
- through works of healing and reconciliation
- through acts of justice and mercy shown to the needy and oppressed
- through any work that is carried out for God's kingdom.

Through the Sacraments each Catholic has a vocation to be a sign and symbol of God's kingdom in the world – in their family life, business life and social life. The *Decree on the Apostolate of Lay People*, published in 1965, underlined the important part that lay people play in spreading the Christian Gospel to the modern world. The Church has only one mission and everyone, lay, religious and ordained, must work together to carry it out.

2 A holy vocation. Down the centuries certain Christian men and women have been 'called' to consecrate themselves to the work of God and his kingdom in a special way. They have taken the three vows, first demanded by St Benedict, of poverty, chastity and obedience and have lived a common life together in community. These communities have included:
- enclosed, contemplative communities
- monastic communities
- communities made up of lay people.

Most of the communities have dedicated themselves to a particular vocation, whether in medical, educational or social work. The vows that they have taken free them from the concerns of this world and give them the opportunity to attach themselves to the One who really matters – Christ. Sometimes ordained priests belong to a particular religious community. These ordained men undertake the work that is specifically associated with the community, including teaching, preaching or missionary work. They return regularly to their community for worship and refreshment. These men, like all priests, have felt the call of God and have responded to follow a life of holy simplicity. In a real way they are following in the footsteps of the early disciples, who left everything to follow Jesus (see Extract 1).

DISCUSSION POINT

What real difference do you think it would make to working people if they believed that their job of work was a calling given to them by God?

WORK TO DO

1 a) What is a vocation?
   b) Give examples of two jobs that you look upon as 'vocations'.
   c) What makes these jobs different from other occupations?

2 Give three examples of different ways of following a Christian vocation.

3 a) Do you think any job can be looked upon as a vocation?
   b) If people looked upon their work, whatever it is, as a vocation, what difference do you think it might make to them?

4 Read Extract 1 carefully. This describes the common vocation to which all true Catholics are called. How would you describe that vocation?

KEY WORDS

Baptism
Confirmation
Eucharist
Holy Communion
Priest
Sacrament
Vocation

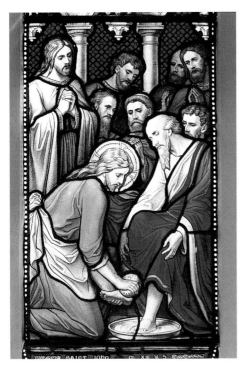

The example of Jesus in washing the feet of his disciples should inspire anyone in a vocation. What do you think they can learn from the action of Jesus?

11.2 HOLY ORDERS

KEY QUESTION

What are holy orders and why are they so important in the Catholic Church?

Extract 1

Let everyone revere the deacons as Jesus Christ, the bishop as the image of the Father, and the presbyters [priests] as the senate of God and the assembly of the apostles. For without them one cannot speak of the Church.

Ignatius, second-century Church leader

Ordained ministers are given a ministry of service to the Catholic community. The ministerial priesthood is different from the common priesthood of all believers (see 11.1) since it encourages and develops the grace bestowed on all believers by Baptism and the other Sacraments.

The sacrament of holy orders

It is through the Sacrament of Holy Orders that Christ continues the ministry in his Church which was begun with the apostles. Through the work of ordained ministers, especially bishops and priests, Christ becomes visibly present to the Church on earth as its head. The ordained priesthood also acts on behalf of the whole Church by leading and directing its worship to God.

Through Ordination men are consecrated to one of the following orders:
- the Episcopacy – bishops
- the Presbyterate – priests
- the Diaconate – deacons.

As Extract 1 shows, this three-fold division goes back to the early centuries of Christianity. The Sacrament of Holy Orders bestows a special gift of the Holy Spirit which enables each person to carry out his new responsibilities. Within the local church community this involves a partnership between the priest and the people. Acting in the place of Christ, the priest moulds and rules the people. For their part the people join in the offering of the Eucharist because they, too, are priests. They demonstrate this through prayer and thanksgiving; by living a holy life of self-denial; and by working for the needs of others.

The Second Vatican Council underlined the importance of all believers in the Church but stressed that bishops, priests and deacons have a particular responsibility to:
- proclaim and teach the word of God to all
- lead the Catholic community in its worship
- exercise leadership over the Catholic community by imitating the example of Jesus in humble and self-denying service.

What do you think are the most important roles played by a priest in a Roman Catholic community?

Bishops, priests and deacons fulfil different roles in the Catholic community.

1 Bishops ('overseers'). The bishop receives the fullness of the Sacrament of Holy Orders – what Church tradition has called the 'high priesthood'. Bishops are the successors of the apostles and so are expected to take Christ's place as teachers, shepherds and priests. In the modern Church the Pope approves the choice of a bishop, who may then be consecrated only by his fellow bishops. This emphasises the 'collegiate' nature of the Church's leadership. Each bishop is responsible for a local area (diocese) as well as being part of the college of bishops which has responsibility for the universal Church.

2 Priests ('elders'). Priests, through ordination, share in the three-fold ministry of Christ – as ministers of God's word, as ministers of the sacraments and as pastoral guides to the Catholic community. Whilst the fullness of the Sacrament of Holy Orders is found in the episcopacy, yet bishops and priests are co-workers (see Extract 2).

3 Deacons. Deacons, who may be married, assist bishops and priests by the ministry of liturgy (taking services); the ministry of the word (preaching) and the ministry of charity (caring for the needy).

Women priests

Women are not admitted to the priesthood of the Roman Catholic Church, although other Churches, notably the Anglican and Nonconformist Churches, do ordain women. As Extract 3 makes clear, the Roman Catholic Church is resolutely committed to maintaining its position. Jesus did not admit any women apostles. Paul taught that women were not permitted to speak in church (1 Corinthians 14:33) nor to exercise any authority over a man (Timothy 2:12). The advice of Scripture and Church tradition are plainly against women priests and the present Pope, John Paul II, has announced that the ban will continue.

WORK TO DO

1 a) What are Holy Orders?
   b) What are the three levels of holy orders?
   c) List three responsibilities carried out by each of these levels in the Church.

2 a) Why does the Roman Catholic Church refuse to ordain women priests?
   b) Do you agree with its position? Give two arguments to support or oppose it.

3 The CCC says: 'Through the Sacrament of Holy Orders priests share in the universal dimensions of the mission Christ entrusted to the apostles.' Read Matthew 28:19,20. Explain what you think 'the universal dimensions of the mission Christ entrusted to the apostles' are.

Extract 2

Because it is joined with the episcopal order the office of priest shares in the authority by which Christ himself builds up and sanctifies (makes holy) and rules his Body [the Church].

CCC (1567)

Extract 3

The Church, in fidelity to the example of the Lord, does not consider itself authorised to admit women to priestly ordination.

Congregation of the Doctrine of the Faith, 1976

DISCUSSION POINT

What qualities do you think a man needs to become a priest?

KEY WORDS

Apostle
Baptism
Bishop
Deacon
Episcopacy
Eucharist
Holy Orders
Holy Spirit
Ordination
Paul
Pope
Priest
Sacraments
Second Vatican Council

11.3
ORDINATION

KEY QUESTION

What is distinctive about the ordination of bishops and priests?

Ordination is the rite of the Church in which the help of God's Spirit is sought for candidates called by God to the offices of bishop, priest and deacon. Ordination points to two fundamental beliefs about the Church and the way it understands itself which are very important:

1 The ministry of the Church is always linked with the work of Jesus and his apostles.

2 Anyone involved in the ministry of the Church must always draw on the strength and guidance of the Holy Spirit.

Extract 1

Since an overseer is entrusted with God's work, he must be blameless – not overbearing, not quick-tempered, not given to drunkenness, not violent, not pursuing dishonest gain. Rather he must be hospitable, one who loves what is good, who is self-controlled, upright, holy and disciplined. He must hold firmly to the trustworthy message as it has been taught, so that he can encourage others by sound doctrine, and refute those who oppose it.

Titus 1:6–9

The ordination of priests and deacons

The ordination of priests and deacons follows a similar pattern. The ordination takes place within the Liturgy of the Eucharist celebrated by the bishop or bishops. Representatives of the diocese should be present, since it is among them that the priest has been called by God to serve.

After the Liturgy of the Word the priests are called forth by name. They are asked whether they wish to serve God's people, to which each candidate replies, 'I am ready and willing'. The bishop obtains confirmation that the priest is suitable to serve the people and the people of God show their approval by applauding and responding with the words 'Thanks be to God'. The bishop then asks for confirmation that each candidate is prepared to:
- care for God's people
- celebrate the sacraments
- preach God's word
- dedicate their life to building up God's kingdom
- obey the bishop, and his successors.

Ordination then takes place. The bishops present lay their hands on the head of each candidate as a special prayer is offered up (see Extract 2). The hands of the priest are anointed with the oil of chrism and the symbols of his office are given to him – vestments, a chalice containing water and wine, and a paten on which rests the bread to be consecrated. The ceremony ends with the exchange of the sign of peace. The liturgy then continues with the newly ordained priest concelebrating the Mass with the bishop and his fellow priests.

Extract 2

Almighty Father, grant to this servant of yours the dignity of priesthood. Renew within him the spirit of holiness. As a co-worker with the order of bishops, may he be faithful to the ministry that he receives from you, Lord God, and be to others a model of right conduct.

Prayer said by the bishop at ordination of priest

The ordination of a bishop

Consecration to the episcopal office as a bishop confers responsibilities given by Christ – to teach, to rule and to sanctify (make holy) the people entrusted to his care. In addition, consecration to the office of bishops also confers a sacred character enabling bishops, as the successors of the apostles, to take Christ's place and represent him in his roles as teacher, shepherd and priest.

In the modern Church bishops must be approved by the Pope and can only be ordained by their fellow bishops. During his ordination the new bishop is given the Gospel-book, his episcopal ring, a mitre, a staff (crozier) and the Bishop's chair. As a successor to the apostles he is expected to act as a good shepherd to those who have been entrusted to his care.

WORK TO DO

1 What is ordination?

2 a) Describe the liturgy by which deacons and priests are ordained into the ministry of the Church.
   b) How does the ordination of a bishop differ from that of a priest or deacon?
   c) What beliefs about the Church and its ministry underlie the liturgy of ordination?

3 The key-note of the ordination of a new priest is that of service – service to God and service to the people.
   a) Describe how this central element of service is brought out in the ordination service.
   b) Describe two ways in which a priest might serve the people amongst whom he is called to work.

4 In Extract 1 Paul describes the kind of person whom he would expect to be appointed an elder (priest). In Extract 2 the bishop prays that God will 'Renew within him [the priest] the spirit of holiness'. Using the extract from Paul as your guide, explain what holy qualities you would expect in a priest.

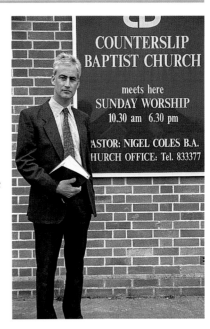

A Baptist minister. Find out the attitude of the Roman Catholic Church towards men and women ordained by other Churches.

DISCUSSION POINT

Why do you think that his ordination into Holy Orders is such an important milestone in the spiritual life of a priest?

Extract 3

Every priest relies on the faith and talents of his parish community . . . The partnership between priest and people is built upon prayer, collaboration and mutual respect and love.

Pope John Paul II

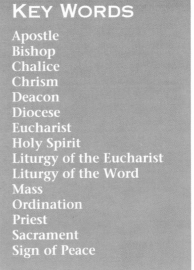

KEY WORDS

Apostle
Bishop
Chalice
Chrism
Deacon
Diocese
Eucharist
Holy Spirit
Liturgy of the Eucharist
Liturgy of the Word
Mass
Ordination
Priest
Sacrament
Sign of Peace

Are you happy with the Roman Catholic Church's refusal to ordain women? Explain your answer.

11.4 RELIGIOUS ORDERS

Religious Orders are communities of Christian men and women who bear witness to the Gospel of Jesus Christ and have pledged themselves to keep the 'Evangelical Counsels' (vows) of obedience, chastity and poverty. People who enter a religious community are usually called nuns, monks or religious priests.

The roots of the monastic movement are found in the fourth century, when groups of men and women moved into the Egyptian desert to dedicate themselves fully to God. Following the example of Jesus, who spent 40 days in the desert, these people began to work out the implications of their baptismal vows in a hostile environment where many conflicts between good and evil took place. To begin with, the people lived as hermits but, before long, they started to live together in religious communities.

KEY QUESTION

What are the main religious Orders and what contribution have they made to the Church?

The Benedictines

St Benedict (480–547) is generally regarded as the father of the monastic movement. The first monastery of Benedictines was formed around 529 at Mount Cassino, some 130 km south of Rome. The 'Rule of St Benedict' was used to organise most of the monastic communities that followed and it emphasised:

- the importance of stability in the community. Monks normally remain in the same monastery from the time they take their vows until they die.
- the importance of a balance within the community between communal prayer, work and relaxation.
- the important role of the abbot, who is elected by the monks themselves. Within the community he is responsible for running the life of the monastery, and especially for ordering worship.
- the three-fold vow that every monk was expected to take – obedience to the abbot, poverty and chastity. You can find out more about this in 11.5.

Why do you think that it is important to strike a balance between religious devotion and work in the monastic life?

Why do you think that the communal life became increasingly important as the monastic movement grew and developed?

The later monastic movement

By the end of the thirteenth century three important religious orders had been established but these were very different from the Benedictines. They were mendicant orders that placed an emphasis on preaching, teaching and living a life of poverty. They were:

- **the Cistercians.** This Order, founded by Bernard of Clairveaux in 1098, called for a spirituality based on personal prayer, devotions and confession, with a strong allegiance to the Virgin Mary.
- **the Franciscans.** Based on the teaching of St Francis of Assisi, the Franciscan Order pioneered a life of simplicity and faithfulness to the Gospel of Christ. Before long an Order of nuns, the Poor Clares, grew up which was also based on Francis' teaching of repentance, trust and respect for the whole of God's creation.
- **the Dominicans.** Founded in 1216, the Dominicans dedicated themselves to a teaching ministry in the Church.

The Missionaries of Charity

One modern religious Order had a greater influence on the Church, and society generally, than any other in the twentieth century. Agnes Gonxha Bojaxhiu joined the Sisters of Loreto, in Ireland, at the age of 17. Within a year she was sent to teach in Calcutta, India. She soon became acquainted with the poor who lived and died on the streets. In 1948 she left the Sisters to work with the sick and dying in the city's slums. She became known as Mother Teresa. In the following year she founded the Missionaries of Charity (an order of sisters, brothers and priests) to serve the poor by providing food, medical help and shelter. Within 30 years there were 80 branches of the Order in 32 different countries. In 1979 Mother Teresa was awarded the Nobel Prize and she died in 1997. By the year 2000 the process leading to her beatification in the Church was well under way. The fact that this was proceeding so quickly was an indication of the respect in the Church, and throughout the world, for the work of Mother Teresa of Calcutta.

WORK TO DO

1 a) How did the monastic way of life begin?
  b) What is the difference between a hermit and a monk?
  c) Why is St Benedict so important in the history of the monastic movement?

2 a) Describe the work of Mother Teresa.
  b) Why do you think that Mother Teresa is held up as a shining example of a modern saint?

3 Why do you think that Christians in the third century made their way out into the desert to give themselves totally to God? Why the desert, in particular?

4 In this unit we mention the Benedictines, the Cistercians, the Franciscans and the Dominicans. Find out enough about one of these Orders to write an essay of about 600 words on it.

Extract 1

[Religious life] is distinguished from other forms of consecrated life by its liturgical character, public profession of the evangelical counsels [of obedience, poverty and chastity], fraternal life led in common, and witness given to the union of Christ with the Church ... Religious life derives from the mystery of the Church. It is a gift she has received from her Lord, a gift she offers as a stable way of life to the faithful called by God to profess the counsels. Thus, the Church can both show forth Christ and acknowledge herself to be the Saviour's bride.

CCC (925)

DISCUSSION POINT

Why do you think that fewer people are hearing the 'religious vocation' today than at any time in the history of the monastic movement?

KEY WORDS

Abbot
Beatification
Chastity
Evangelical Counsel
Hermit
Monastery
Monk
Nun
Priest

11.5 THE EVANGELICAL COUNSELS

The Evangelical Counsels (vows) are gifts given by God to the Church through which individual members of monastic orders, by devoting their lives to the Counsels, build up the Catholic Church in a special way. The three Evangelical Counsels are obedience, chastity and poverty – the vows taken by men and women who devote themselves to the religious life (see 11.4).

KEY QUESTION

What are the evangelical counsels and what part do they play in religious life?

Poverty

Poverty is the first of the Evangelical Counsels which traditionally form the basis of the religious life. By taking up a life of poverty, a person is following the clear example of Jesus, who consistently taught that anyone who wished to enter God's kingdom must be willing to renounce their possessions and family (see Extract 1). The life of complete dependence on God which Jesus followed left him completely open to meet the needs of others. It was the life that the apostles, and other followers of Jesus, sought to imitate in the early years of the fledgling Church after Jesus had gone back to his Father in heaven. Luke tells us that: 'They [the followers of Jesus] devoted themselves to the apostles' teaching and to the fellowship, to the breaking of bread and to prayer . . . All the believers were together and had everything in common.' (Acts 2:42,44).

When monastic living began the prime aim of monks, nuns and hermits was to live by the same principles, and create the same communal life. A life of poverty is fundamental to this vision because it fosters a spirit of total dependence on God, detachment from the goods and pleasures of this life and communion with other Christians. Francis of Assisi (d.1226) gave special meaning to the idea of poverty through the Franciscan order which he founded. Franciscans devote themselves to a life of poverty and simplicity so that they can serve the poor.

Extract 1

As Jesus started on his way, a man ran up to him and fell on his knees before him. 'Good teacher,' he asked, 'what must I do to inherit eternal life?' . . . Jesus looked at him and loved him. 'One thing you lack,' he said. 'Go, sell everything you have and give to the poor and you shall have treasure in heaven. Then come, follow me.'

Mark 10:17,21

Chastity

The second Evangelical Counsel is the virtue that moderates sexual desire. Those who enter monasteries and convents take a vow of chastity. The purpose of this vow is to free those in religious Orders from family responsibilities, so leaving them open to the demands made on them by God and others. As far as we know, Jesus was freed from these responsibilities and so was able to devote himself fully to the building up of God's kingdom on earth. Roman Catholic priests also take the vow of chastity (celibacy) for the same reason. Until the time of the Second Vatican Council it was thought that those in religious and holy Orders were given a higher vocation than those lay people who were married, but this Church Council underlined the sacred vocation of marriage. Everyone, whatever their calling, has a vocation to make Christ known in the situation in which God has placed them.

Why is the life of poverty so important to a nun?

How did the Second Vatican Council balance the importance of the monastic and married vocations?

Obedience

The third Evangelical Counsel draws our attention to the important part played by obedience to the will of God in the life of Jesus. In his case obedience was demanded all the way through to his death on the cross. Through that death salvation became possible for the whole human race. All authority ultimately comes from God. For this reason obedience to human authority is a test of our obedience to God. Paul made this clear on more than one occasion: 'Slaves, obey your earthly masters with respect and fear, and with sincerity of heart, just as you would obey Christ' (Ephesians 6:5).

Within a religious community, authority is invested in those appointed, or elected, to lead the community. By entering a community, and accepting its discipline, a person is placing himself or herself under the discipline of the Abbot or Mother superior. To do so challenges a person's natural pride and so the acceptance of this is a very important spiritual discipline.

WORK TO DO

1 Members of Religious Orders take a voluntary vow of obedience. Why do you think that this vow is important to their religious life?

2 a) What is chastity?
   b) Why do you think that the vow of chastity is important in the religious life of those entering a convent or a monastery?

3 a) How did Jesus set an example to those taking a vow of poverty?
   b) What does the vow of poverty involve?

DISCUSSION POINT

Do you think that keeping the three Evangelical Counsels should be at the heart of the religious life today, or are other things more important?

Extract 2

Observing the evangelical counsels is an answer to: '. . . a divine call to live for God alone, not only by dying to sin but also by renouncing the standards of the world. Religions have handed over their entire lives to God's service in an act of special consecration deeply rooted in their baptismal consecration and which provides an ampler manifestation of it.'

Second Vatican Council

KEY WORDS

Abbot
Apostle
Chastity
Church Council
Evangelical Counsel
Hermit
Monk
Mother Superior
Nun
Paul
Second Vatican Council
Vocation

11.6 THE LAITY

KEY QUESTION

What part does the laity play in the modern Roman Catholic Church?

The laity are those baptised Roman Catholics who are not ordained as priests and who do not belong to a recognised Religious Order. Constituting over 98 per cent of the worldwide Catholic family, the laity are consecrated to God through the three Sacraments of Initiation – Baptism, Confirmation and the Eucharist.

The role of the laity

As we saw in 11.5, the Second Vatican Council gave the laity in the Church equal importance with the clergy and the religious. The quotation from *Lumen Gentium*, the Dogmatic Constitution of the Church, published by the Council (see Extract 1) shows that the laity can expect to share in the three roles performed by Christ. The same three roles for the laity are taken up and expanded in the CCC.

1 A priestly role. Undertakings in family and married life, daily work and leisure are all spiritual sacrifices that are acceptable when offered up to God. In the celebration of the Eucharist these can be offered to God along with the body of Christ. Those possessing the necessary qualities can also offer themselves to work in their local church as lectors (people who give the first or second readings at Mass) or acolytes (people who assist the bishop, priest or deacon in distributing the bread and wine at Mass).

2 A prophetic role. St Thomas Aquinas wrote: 'To teach in order to lead others to faith is the task of every preacher and of each believer.' Lay people are called to be witnesses and to be involved in proclaiming the Gospel of Christ (evangelisation). Lay people are called by God to be evangelists amid the ordinary circumstances of life.

3 A kingly role. By being obedient even to death, Jesus gave to his followers final victory over sin. By working together, lay people can have a great influence on those aspects of life which encourage people to sin. By working with their pastors the laity can also offer themselves in service to their local church.

These three roles underline the teaching of the Catholic Church that the laity has an essential, and central, role to play in the ministry of the modern Church. This was underlined back in 1946 by Pope Pius XII (see Extract 2). It was further emphasised in 1987 when the Church held a World Synod on the Laity. This Synod, in its final document, stressed that the clergy, the religious and the laity were of equal importance in the Church. It saw the special responsibility of the laity as being one of ministry to the world through the ordinary circumstances of family and business life. It also called on the Church to extend the opportunities given to lay people to work and serve in the local church. In particular, it underlined the importance of:

- the vocation given to everyone through baptism.
- the universal call given to everyone, religious and lay, to live a life of holiness. A 1978 document underlined the part that bishops must play in making this possible: 'The Bishop, by virtue of his very ministry, is held to account for the growth in holiness of all his faithful.'

Extract 1

The faithful who by Baptism are incorporated into Christ, are placed in the People of God, and in their own way share the priestly, prophetic and kingly office of Christ, and to the best of their ability carry on the mission of the whole Christian people in the Church and in the world.

Lumen Gentium, *a document resulting from the Second Vatican Council*

Extract 2

[The laity are] in the front line of Church life . . . they, in particular, ought to have an ever-clearer consciousness of belonging to the Church, that is to say, the community of the faithful on earth under the leadership of the Pope, the common Head, and of the bishops in communion with them. They are the Church.

Pope Pius XII, 1946

- the spiritual gifts given to everyone and the need to have an opportunity to use them.
- the need to build up a lay-centred Church with more decisions being taken locally.

This emphasis on the contribution that ordinary church members should be encouraged to make marks a return to the life of the early Christian Church, in which everyone was encouraged to play their part in the spread of the Christian Gospel. The same call is being made by the modern Catholic Church.

WORK TO DO

1 According to the CCC the laity can share in the three roles of Christ.
   a) Who are the laity in the Catholic Church?
   b) What are the three roles of Christ?
   c) Explain how the laity can share in one of these roles.

2 a) Explain how the Church now sees the role of lay people in its life and worship.
   b) How do you think that lay people might look upon their family and business responsibilities as a clear vocation given to them by God?

3 Describe what the World Synod of the Laity, which met in 1987, had to say about the role of lay people in the modern Catholic Church.

DISCUSSION POINT

Why do you think that the modern Catholic Church stresses the role of the laity so heavily?

Extract 3

To teach in order to lead others to faith is the task of every preacher, of each believer . . . The laity can also feel called . . . to cooperate with their pastors in the service of the ecclesial [church] community, for the sake of its growth and life.

CCC (904, 910)

KEY WORDS

Baptism
Bishop
Confirmation
Deacon
Eucharist
Laity
Mass
Priest
Sacraments of Initiation
Second Vatican Council
Vocation

What name is given to those who assist the priest in giving communion?

Why do you think the Church is so dependent on those who give their time freely to its work?

GLOSSARY

Abbot: The leader of a male monastic order.

Abortion: The termination of a pregnancy, involving the destruction of the foetus.

Absolution: The declaration by the priest that a person's sins have been forgiven by God.

Acts of the Apostles: The fifth book in the New Testament, which takes up the story of the Early Church from the Day of Pentecost to the death of Paul.

Adultery: Sexual relations between two people who are not married to each other.

Advent: The start of the Church year, the four-week season leading up to the celebration of Christmas.

Agnus Dei: 'The Lamb of God', Latin title for the litany sung just before the Mass is celebrated.

Almsgiving: An offering made to help those in need.

Altar: The stone or wooden platform at the east end of a church; the priest stands in front of the altar to carry out the Mass.

Anglican Church: The worldwide communion of Churches based on the teachings of the Church of England.

Annulment: The declaration by the Catholic Church that a real marriage did not take place, which leaves the couple free to remarry.

Anti-semitism: Hatred directed specifically against Jewish people.

Apartheid: Separation of the races, a policy adopted by successive governments in South Africa from 1948 to 1994.

Apostle: One of the twelve disciples of Jesus; the name given to them on the Day of Pentecost.

Apostles' Creed: The statement of Christian belief originally thought to have come directly from the apostles, now thought to have been written sometime in the fourth century.

Baptism: The Catholic rite of initiation into the Church carried out on babies or, occasionally, adults.

Beatification: The second step in the process of a person becoming a saint in the Catholic Church.

Beatitudes: The statements of Jesus, found in Matthew 5–7, about the spiritual state of the truly happy person.

Bishop: The highest of the three orders in the Catholic priesthood (the others being deacon and priest).

Celibacy: The acceptance of the unmarried state by a priest or a member of a religious order, as a vocation from God.

Chalice: The cup used for the wine and the blood of Jesus at the Mass.

Chastity: One of the three Evangelical Counsels, which excludes any kind of sexual activity for those who take the vow.

Chrism: The consecrated oil used in the Catholic Church for different sacraments.

Chrismation: The service in the Orthodox Church which brings together Baptism and Confirmation.

Church Council: A gathering of bishops and the Pope; the last Church Council was the Second Vatican Council.

Church of England: The established Church in England, formed in the sixteenth century after it broke away from the Catholic Church.

Communion of Saints: The fellowship of each Christian with Christ and, through him, with all saints past and present.

Confirmation: The service which admits a person into full membership of the Catholic Church.

Consecration: The moment in the Mass when the bread and wine become the body and blood of Christ.

Creed: An official statement of Christian belief; the Nicene and the Apostles' Creeds are used in Catholic churches.

Day of Pentecost: The birthday of the Christian Church, the day on which the Holy Spirit was given to the first disciples.

Deacon: An ordained man, who can be a lay person or someone who is going to become a priest after a year.

Diocese: The area over which a bishop has authority, which is further divided into parishes.

Disciple: Someone who accepts the discipline of a religious teacher; Jesus chose twelve disciples, later called apostles.

Easter: The festival at which Christians remember the death and resurrection of Jesus.

Easter Vigil: The service held between sunset on Holy Saturday and dawn on Easter Sunday.

Episcopacy: The office of bishops within the Catholic Church.

Epistle: A letter in the New Testament: written by Paul, Peter and John, amongst others.

Eucharist: 'Thanksgiving', the sacrifice of Jesus celebrated on the altar, also known as the Mass.

Eucharistic Prayer: The prayer which is found at the heart of the Eucharist.

Euthanasia: 'Easy death', the ending of a person's life with their consent.

Evangelical counsels: The three vows of poverty, chastity and obedience taken by someone entering a monastic order.

Extreme Unction: The anointing of a person with oil as death approaches.

Fall: The belief that the first man and woman gave in to temptation in the Garden of Eden, leading to original sin which affects everyone.

Fornication: Sexual relationships outside marriage.

Gentile: A person who is not a Jew.

Gloria: The hymn used in the Mass which begins 'Glory to God in the highest'.

Good Friday: The day on which Christians remember the death of Jesus.

Gospels: The four accounts at the beginning of the New Testament of the life and death of Jesus.

Hermit: A man or a woman who seeks God by living a solitary life, and having only minimal contact with other human beings.

Heterosexual: Someone who is sexually attracted to members of the opposite sex.

Holy Communion: The most important service in most Christian Churches, at which worshippers remember the death of Jesus by eating bread and drinking wine together.

Holy Orders: The office and authority required by those who are ordained to administer the Sacraments.

Holy Spirit: The third member of the Christian Trinity, the power of God active in today's world.

Holy Thursday: The day before Good Friday, the day on which Jesus ate his last meal with his disciples, also known as Maundy Thursday.

Homily: A sermon given by a priest or deacon during the Liturgy of the Word.

Homosexuality: The preference that some people have for sexual relationships with members of their own sex.

Hospice: A system of care which offers people who are dying real control over their pain and a dignified death.

Host: The name given to the altar bread used during the Mass; also called the Body of Christ.

Indulgence: The punishment of a person so that he or she can enter more fully into the forgiveness of God.

Infant Baptism: The sprinkling of children with holy water, as an initiation into membership of the Catholic Church.

John the Baptist: The prophet sent by God to prepare the people for the coming of Jesus; also known as the Forerunner.

Laity: Any member of a congregation who is not ordained.

Last Supper: The last meal that Jesus ate with his disciples, which provides the model on which the Mass is based.

Lectern: The place from which the Word of God, the Bible, is read in a church.

Lectionary: The book of Bible readings used for Mass.

Lent: The season of 40 days of reflection running from Ash Wednesday to Good Friday, traditionally a time of fasting.

Lesbian: A woman who is sexually attracted to other women.

Liturgy: The public and official prayer and rites of the Church.

Liturgy of the Eucharist: The second part of the Mass, which includes the sharing of the bread and wine.

Liturgy of the Word: The first part of the Mass, which contains Bible readings from the Old Testament, Epistles and Gospels, together with a homily.

Lord's Prayer: The prayer that Jesus taught his disciples, used in all Catholic Services.

Mass: The offering of the body and blood of Christ by the priest on behalf of the people.

Methodist Church: The Protestant Church formed in the eighteenth century based on the teachings of John Wesley.

Miracle: A change in a situation brought about by the direct intervention of God.

Monastery: A house where a group of men live the monastic life together.

Monk: A male member of a religious Order who lives in a monastery.

Mortal sin: A 'death-dealing' sin which is very serious.

Mother Superior: The traditional name for the head of a female religious order.

Natural family planning: Ways of preventing conception after sexual intercourse without using any artificial methods.

New Testament: The second part of the Bible, which contains four Gospels (Matthew, Mark, Luke and John) and many Epistles (letters).

Nicene Creed: The Creed drawn up by the Council of bishops which met at Nicea in 325.

Nun: A member of a female religious Order who lives in a convent.

Old Testament: The first part of the Bible, containing 39 books, which also forms the Jewish Scriptures.

Ordination: The ritual by which lay people are admitted to the priesthood of the Roman Catholic Church; the service in which priests become bishops.

Original Sin: The Catholic belief that all people are born with a tendency to sin because of the first sin committed by Adam and Eve.

Orthodox Church: The Church which separated from the Roman Catholic Church in the Great Schism of 1054.

Pacifism: The belief that it is wrong for a Christian to use violence in any situation.

Parable: A story told by Jesus which carries a strong religious and moral lesson.

Paschal Candle: The large candle which stands in the sanctuary from the Easter Vigil until Pentecost.

Paschal Mystery: The total event of Christ's passion including his death, resurrection, ascension and the sending of God's Holy Spirit.

Passover: The Jewish festival that celebrates the release of the Israelites from slavery in Egypt.

Paul: An early apostle, who was converted on the road to Damascus, wrote many letters in the New Testament and founded many first-century churches.

Penance: A penalty given to someone by a priest to demonstrate that they are sorry for a sinful action.

Pentecost Sunday: The day, 40 days after Easter Sunday, on which Christians remember the giving of the Holy Spirit to the first disciples.

Peter: The most prominent of the disciples of Jesus, the first Bishop of Rome and Pope.

Pope: 'Papa', the head of the Roman Catholic Church, successor of St Peter, capable of speaking infallibly (without error).

Priest: A man with authority to administer the sacraments through his ordination to the priesthood.

Prophets: One section of the Jewish Scriptures, the other two being the Torah (Books of the Law) and the Writings.

Protestant: Collective name for those Churches which broke away from the Roman Catholic Church during the sixteenth-century Reformation.

Psalm: A collection of songs in the Jewish Scriptures which are used in Christian worship.

Purgatory: A state between earth and heaven where those who have died in God's grace work out their minor sins and faults.

Quakers: A name for members of the Society of Friends, a group formed in the seventeenth century, based on the teachings of George Fox.

Rabbi: A Jewish teacher.

Sabbath day: The Jewish holy day runs for the 25 hours from sunset on Friday.

Sacrament: A 'Sacred Mystery', one of the seven rituals recognised by the Roman Catholic Church as bringing God within the reach of human experience.

Sacrament of Reconciliation: The sacrament which offers forgiveness for those who acknowledge and repent of their sins.

Saint: A man or a woman who is honoured because of the holiness of their lives.

Salvation Army: A Protestant organisation founded by William and Catherine Booth in 1880, distinctive because of its uniform.

Sanctus: The part of the Mass which begins 'Holy, Holy, Holy'.

Satan: The 'adversary' or 'enemy', the opposer of God in both the Old and New Testaments.

Second Coming: The belief of Christians that Jesus will return to earth again to set up his kingdom.

Second Vatican Council: The council of bishops of the Catholic Church, held in Rome between 1962 and 1965.

Sermon on the Mount: A collection of the teachings of Jesus, found in Matthew 5–7.

Sign of the Cross: The tracing of the cross shape on the body at certain important moments in Catholic devotion.

Sign of Peace: The moment in the Mass when members of the congregation greet each other and wish each other God's blessing.

Son of Man: The favourite description of Jesus for himself.

Sunday: The day on which Jesus rose from the dead, adopted by Christians as their holy day early in the fourth century.

Synagogue: A Jewish place of worship.

Synoptic Gospels: The name given to the first three Gospels (Matthew, Mark and Luke) because they have much material in common; 'seeing-together'.

Temple: The place of Jewish worship in Jerusalem, first built by King Solomon, rebuilt by King Herod the Great and finally destroyed by the Romans in 70 CE.

Ten Commandments: The laws which lie at the heart of the Torah and spell out a person's responsibilities to God and their fellow human beings.

Torah: The first five books of the Old Testament (Genesis, Exodus, Leviticus, Deuteronomy and Numbers), the most sacred part of their Scriptures to all Jews.

Tridium: The three days prior to Easter Sunday (Holy Thursday, Good Friday and Holy Saturday).

Trinity: The Christian belief that there are three Persons (God the Father, God the Son and God the Holy Spirit) in the one God.

Venial sin: A less serious sin that can be forgiven after confession.

Viaticum: 'Food for the journey', the last Communion given before a person dies.

Virgin Mary: The mother of Jesus, venerated by Roman Catholics.

Vocation: 'Calling', someone called by God to carry out a special task.

Whitsun: 'White Sunday', another name for Pentecost.

Writings: The last group of books in the Jewish Scriptures, after the Torah and the Prophets.

INDEX